W9-AJS-500

YOU'LL NEVER LOOK AT THE NEWS THE SAME WAY AGAIN!

NATIONAL
GEOGRAPHIC
KiDS

weird but true!

RIPPED
FROM THE
HEADLINES 2

REAL-LIFE STORIES
YOU HAVE TO READ TO
BELIEVE

NATIONAL GEOGRAPHIC

WASHINGTON, D.C.

TABLE OF CONTENTS

INTRODUCTION

NEWS GOT YOU FEELIN' THE BLUES? Think nonfiction is nonfun? Well then get ready for your mind to be blown! *Weird But True!: Ripped From the Headlines 2* is here, and it's odder than ever! Just like the first edition, this volume has all the things you'd expect in a newspaper—world news, sports and science sections, entertainment stories, and more—but with a twist. Everything in these pages is factual, freaky, funny, bizarre, bold, and brain busting. In other words, totally weird but true!

Did you know that animals have run for political office? That students have sent a rubber chicken into space? Have you heard about the new glow-in-the-dark roads? These are just a few of the awesome action-packed stories you'll find featured in this

KING CUBED
PAGES 166–167

book. But that's not all! Catch a glimpse of the real-life Spider-Man who climbs cliffs without using ropes. Speaking of superheroes, how about the caped crusader who patrols the streets of Seattle, Washington, U.S.A., looking for criminals to capture? If daring is more your scene, check out the flying car, take a bite out of the world's spiciest pizza, or dip your toe into the world's most crowded swimming pool. Need a dose of sweet? No problem. Check into the totally panda-themed hotel, cuddle a baby aardvark, or set your sights on a replica of the Sistene Chapel made out of candy!

From animals to athletes, space to space-age technology, these news stories will open your eyes to the weird side of this wonderful world.

Whether you're reading about bug buffets, shape-shifting buildings, zombie ants, or ostrich races, one thing's for sure—you'll never look at the news the same way again!

CHAPTER 1

WACKY
WORLD
HEADLINES

DENTS SEND CHICKEN INTO SPACE • SUPERSIZE W
ANT SNOWBALL DAMAGES DORM • GIRL MISTAKE
• LOOSE LEOPARD SHUTS DOWN TOWN • CASTA
BY TRIKE! • REAL-LIFE SUPERHERO RESCUE • RO

STUDENTS SEND, CHICKEN SKY-HIGH, PAGE 27

ROLLING STONES WRECK COUNTRYSIDE

TRENTINO-ALTO ADIGE, ITALY

LIVING IN THE MOUNTAINS CAN BE BEAUTIFUL—and dangerous! This massive boulder was one of two that tumbled onto this property after breaking loose from nearby cliffs. The boulders may have begun their descent as a single chunk of rock before breaking into smaller pieces. One wiped out a barn and several rows of grapevines before rolling to a halt. Despite all the damage, the homeowners were lucky: One of the boulders stopped just three feet (1 m) from their house!

CATS CAUGHT UP IN MINI-TWISTER

CATNADO!

CHOBHAM, ENGLAND

It sounds like a scene from *The Wizard of Oz:* Four feral cats took a ride on a mini-tornado as it swept across a farm in rural England. Though the cats were lifted six feet (1.8 m) off the ground, they came through their airborne adventure unharmed.

REAL-LIFE SUPERHERO RESCUE!

WHO BATMAN AND CAPTAIN AMERICA

WHAT RESCUED A CAT FROM A BURNING HOME

WHERE MILTON, WEST VIRGINIA, U.S.A.

HOW WHILE ENTERTAINING CHILDREN AT A PARTY, BATMAN AND CAPTAIN AMERICA NOTICED A NEARBY HOME ON FIRE. THE SUPERHEROES KICKED IN THE DOOR TO RESCUE A CAT TRAPPED INSIDE.

OUTCOME AFTER RECEIVING MOUTH-TO-MOUTH RESUSCITATION FROM BATMAN, THE CAT REGAINED CONSCIOUSNESS AND SWIPED AT ITS RESCUER'S FACE. THANKS TO SUPERHEROES, THIS CAT'S STILL GOT NINE LIVES LEFT TO LIVE.

NEWS FEED

>>> **KALYAN, INDIA:** POLICE OFFICERS HAD TO GET CREATIVE WHEN A THIEF SNATCHED A GOLD CHAIN AND THEN SWALLOWED IT FOR SAFEKEEPING:

RUDOLPH ROCKS A NEW LOOK

LAPLAND, FINLAND

Reindeer herders in Europe's far north are trying to make their livestock easier for drivers to spot—and to avoid. The animals rubbed off reflective tape placed on their antlers, so herders next turned to reflective paint. It worked: In tests, the paint was able to withstand the region's harsh, cold climate. Now entire herds may sport the bright idea.

CORVETTE CAR-TASTROPHE!

BOWLING GREEN, KENTUCKY, U.S.A.

Eight Corvettes plunged nearly 30 feet (9 m) when a sinkhole suddenly opened up inside the National Corvette Museum. Typically formed by water wearing away rock, sinkholes riddle Kentucky's karst region. Workers spent several weeks stabilizing the edge of the opening before they could fish out the cars to assess the damage.

THEY FED HIM 96 BANANAS TO HURRY ALONG THE GOLD'S EXIT SO IT COULD BE RETURNED TO ITS RIGHTFUL OWNER!

VOTERS KNOW NOT WHOM THEY SUPPORT

1938

Boston Curtis, a brown mule, was elected precinct committeeman in Milton, Washington, U.S.A. But none of the 51 people who voted for Curtis knew he was a mule until after the election! The stunt was created by Milton's mayor to show that sometimes voters support candidates they know nothing about.

A VOTE TO PRESERVE RABBIT HASH

2004

Junior the black Lab beat out another dog, a pig, and a donkey to become mayor of Rabbit Hash, Kentucky, U.S.A. The town's odd election was for a good cause: Each vote cost one dollar, with all of the money going toward repairing Rabbit Hash's historic buildings.

>>> PAW-LITICIANS: ANIMALS FOR OFFICE

1959

ANCIENT GREEKS *CAST THEIR VOTES* BY PLACING A **PEBBLE** IN AN URN.

BETTER TO ELECT A RHINO

Frustrated residents of São Paulo, Brazil, decided the humans on the ballot weren't worth voting for. So nearly 100,000 people instead wrote in the name of a rhinoceros! Cacareco, on loan to the São Paulo Zoo, beat out 11 opposing parties. Despite her victory, she wasn't allowed to take office.

Support
Tuxedo Stan
Because neglect isn't working

www.tuxedostan.com

NEGLECT ISN'T WORKING

2012

Tuxedo Stan found a home—and a purpose. The former stray cat ran for mayor of Halifax, Nova Scotia, Canada, on a campaign that promised to provide better conditions for cats. Though he wasn't elected (the city bans animals from holding office), non-feline politicians made changes to improve life for strays anyway.

RESIDENTS OF **TASMANIA, AUSTRALIA,** CAN **VOTE** FROM THEIR *CELL PHONES.*

TIRED OF VOTING FOR RATS? VOTE FOR A CAT

2013

When Morris the cat ran for mayor of Xalapa, Mexico, the candidate highlighted his extensive experience lazing about (just like politicians, Morris's owner said) and promised to donate leftover kitty litter to fill potholes in the streets.

MORRIS

15

CRAZY
CLOSE CALLS

CASTAWAY TURNS UP 8,000 MILES, 14 MONTHS LATER
(12,900 km)

MARSHALL ISLANDS

After spending 14 months adrift on the Pacific Ocean, Jose Salvador Alvarenga finally washed ashore—8,000 miles (12,900 km) from where he started! Alvarenga went fishing off the coast of Mexico in late November 2012. On January 30, 2014, his boat beached on a coral atoll in the remote Marshall Islands. Residents came to his aid and communicated with him through an islander who had learned Spanish by watching *Dora the Explorer*. Alvarenga explained that he had drifted across the Pacific Ocean after being blown off course and caught in a storm. He said he survived by catching and eating fish, birds, and turtles.

THE **MARSHALL ISLANDS** ARE ON AVERAGE ONLY **7 FEET** ABOVE **(2 m) SEA LEVEL.**

NEWS FEED

NEWFOUNDLAND, CANADA: WHAT A CANADIAN MAN THOUGHT WAS A BEACHED WHALE TURNED OUT TO BE A GREENLAND SHARK—CHOKING ON A MOOSE!

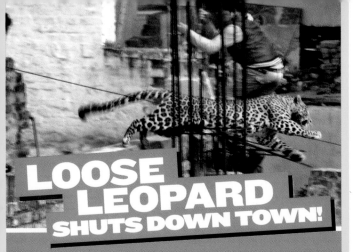

LOOSE LEOPARD SHUTS DOWN TOWN!

MEERUT, INDIA

Students in India got a day off after a leopard wandered into a busy urban area. Seeking to escape a crowd of taunting onlookers, the wild cat entered a hospital, where it sparked panic among patients and staff. The leopard then leaped through a hole in the wall and raced through the city, visiting a movie theater and an apartment building before disappearing. Concerned about the cat's whereabouts, officials closed markets and schools and urged people to stay home for the rest of the day.

LEOPARDS CAN **LIVE** JUST ABOUT **ANYWHERE,** INCLUDING **RAIN FORESTS** AND **DESERTS.**

THE FIRST **COWS** ARRIVED IN THE *UNITED STATES* IN THE **EARLY 1600S** WITH THE SETTLERS AT JAMESTOWN, VIRGINIA.

GASSY COWS BLOW OFF BARN ROOF

RASDORF, GERMANY

Who knew flatulence could be so dangerous? A barn housing 90 cows caught fire after it gradually filled with methane, a flammable gas released in livestock toots and burps. Such gassy behavior is normal for cows, which each emit between 176 and 243 pounds (80–110 kg) of methane per day. Exactly why the gas built up inside the barn remains unclear. But police blamed a static electric charge for igniting it. Though the roof went up in flames, the cows were largely unharmed.

HE ENLISTED ANOTHER MAN TO HELP PULL THE OVERSIZE MEAL OUT OF THE SHARK'S MOUTH AND PUSH THE FISH BACK INTO THE WATER.

GIRL
MISTAKEN FOR
STUFFED UNICORN

ANTALYA, TURKEY

Airport customs can be crazy. But not even long lines can excuse this mix-up: A girl from southern Wales was allowed into Turkey after showing her stuffed unicorn's DesignaBear passport instead of her own! Her mother accidentally handed the immigration officer the wrong passport. Rather than ask for the right one, the officer simply stamped the passport for the plush pal—which wasn't even along for the trip!

GUESS WHICH ONE IS THE UNICORN

SUPERSIZE WASP NEST FOUND IN HOME

WHO MILLIONS OF WASPS

WHAT BUILT A 22-FOOT (7-M) NEST INSIDE AN EMPTY VACATION HOME

WHERE TENERIFE, CANARY ISLANDS, SPAIN

HOW THE WASPS, THOUGHT TO HAVE MIGRATED MORE THAN 60 MILES (100 KM) FROM AFRICA, SETTLED INTO THE EMPTY HOUSE AND BUILT AN EVER GROWING STRUCTURE AS THE COLONY EXPANDED.

OUTCOME BY THE TIME NEIGHBORS CALLED THE POLICE, THE NEST NEARLY FILLED ONE ROOM OF THE HOUSE. POLICE WERE SEARCHING FOR THE HOME'S OWNER TO TAKE CARE OF THE PROBLEM.

NEWS FEED

>>> **ANDERSLÖV, SWEDEN:** BLOND SWEDES FOUND THEIR HAIR GOING GREEN AFTER MOVING INTO NEW HOMES. THE CULPRIT: UNTREATED COPPER WATER

GIANT SNOWBALL DAMAGES DORM

PORTLAND, OREGON, U.S.A.

Take some 800 pounds (363 kg) of snow and a steep hill, and what do you get? A cracked wall. Students at Reed College built a 40-inch (1-m) snowball that rolled downhill—and right into a dorm, startling those inside. The snowball builders—both math majors—apparently miscalculated their ability to control the beastly ball of ice.

FAKE GORILLA CAUGHT IN ZOO

TOKYO, JAPAN

Visitors at Tokyo's Ueno Zoo gawked with surprise as workers wrangled a runaway gorilla—a fake one, that is. A costumed zoo employee pretended to be an escaped ape as part of an annual drill to practice catching animals on the loose.

THIS IS ONLY A DRILL!

PIPES. HOT WATER STRIPPED OFF THE COPPER, WHICH THEN DYED THE SWEDES' HAIR WHEN WASHED.

SOUTH POLE BY TRIKE!

WELSH WOMAN FIRST TO ACCOMPLISH FRIGID FEAT

ANTARCTICA

Wind, snow, and subzero temperatures—do these sound like perfect conditions for a ride? Maria Leijerstam of Wales thought so. She became the first person to cycle from the edge of the Antarctic continent to the South Pole, a journey of nearly 400 miles (638 km). Completing her trip in just 10 days, 14 hours, and 56 minutes, she beat out two other cyclists attempting the feat at the same time.

Leijerstam began preparing for her Antarctic adventure four years before she ever reached the starting line. She cycled for hours each day to train her body. She recruited experts to help plan her course and to build the Polar Cycle, a fat-tired recumbent (back-leaning) tricycle she designed for her expedition. The low profile and extra wheel on this one-of-a-kind trike helped keep Leijerstam on the move in Antarctica's powerful winds.

To reach the welcome sight of the South Pole, Leijerstam battled more than snowdrifts and extreme cold (as if those weren't enough). Her route included an uphill, high-elevation climb that topped out at more than 9,600 feet (2,926 m). And she was forced to detour around a dangerous region riddled with deep cracks in the ice.

THE WARMEST TEMPERATURE EVER RECORDED AT THE SOUTH POLE WAS **9.9 DEGREES** FAHRENHEIT (-12.3 degrees Celsius).

AN AMERICAN MAN SPENT **MORE THAN 3 HOURS** RIDING HIS BIKE UNDERWATER, *SETTING A RECORD DISTANCE OF 1.89 MILES* (3.04 km).

FROSTY FACE OF
DETERMINATION

CELEBRATING AT
THE FINISH POLE

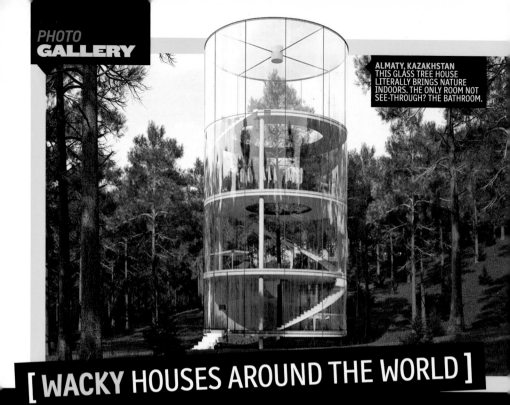

ALMATY, KAZAKHSTAN
THIS GLASS TREE HOUSE
LITERALLY BRINGS NATURE
INDOORS. THE ONLY ROOM NOT
SEE-THROUGH? THE BATHROOM.

[WACKY HOUSES AROUND THE WORLD]

Tired of cookie-cutter homes? Consider what it would be like to live in one of these houses, which are anything but average!

THE
**KERET
HOUSE**
SITS
ATOP
STILTS.

WARSAW, POLAND
ONLY 48 INCHES
(122 CM) AT ITS
WIDEST POINT AND
SQUEEZED INTO
AN ALLEY, THE
KERET HOUSE IS A
TEMPORARY HOME
FOR TRAVELING
WRITERS,
INCLUDING ITS
NAMESAKE,
ETGAR KERET.

PÓVOA DE VARZIM, PORTUGAL THE FOLDING ALUMINUM SHUTTERS COVERING THIS HOME HELP IT BEAT THE SUMMER HEAT. SHAPES CUT INTO THE SHUTTERS STILL LET LIGHT IN, THOUGH.

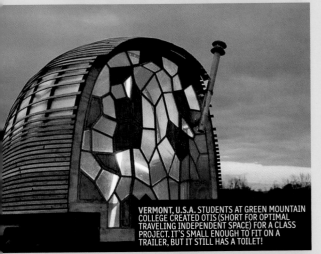

VERMONT, U.S.A. STUDENTS AT GREEN MOUNTAIN COLLEGE CREATED OTIS (SHORT FOR OPTIMAL TRAVELING INDEPENDENT SPACE) FOR A CLASS PROJECT. IT'S SMALL ENOUGH TO FIT ON A TRAILER, BUT IT STILL HAS A TOILET!

THE TOILET
IN OTIS
COMPOSTS
OCCUPANTS'
WASTE!

WALES TWO PEOPLE BUILT THE HOBBIT-LIKE UNDERCROFT HOME IN JUST A FEW MONTHS FROM MATERIALS MOSTLY FOUND ON THE PROPERTY.

OFF-THE-WALL ART

VANCOUVER, BRITISH COLUMBIA, CANADA

IT'S A BIRD! IT'S A PLANE! IT'S ... ART! Designed by artist Janet Echelman, this 745-foot (230-m) sculpture dangling over downtown Vancouver stopped people in their tracks. Made from fibers 15 times stronger than steel, "Skies Painted With Unnumbered Sparks" served as a canvas for a kaleidoscope of light beamed from a ground-based device. With the help of digital artist Aaron Koblin, passersby could add their own artistic flourishes by using their smartphones.

OUT-OF-THIS-WORLD MUSIC VIDEO

INTERNATIONAL SPACE STATION
Canadian astronaut Chris Hadfield made a music video about 250 miles (400 km) above Earth's surface! While floating aboard the International Space Station, Hadfield strummed his trusty guitar and belted out David Bowie's song "Space Oddity." His recorded performance was later beamed to millions of enthusiastic Earthlings. Space oddity, indeed!

ANSWER: **B.** Cosmonauts consider it bad luck to watch the rocket as it is rolled to the launchpad!

STUDENTS SEND CHICKEN SKY-HIGH

CALIFORNIA, U.S.A.

Space-loving students in California knew just what to do when they learned the sun would soon unleash a particularly strong burst of energy. They sent a rubber chicken right into the intense solar radiation to record it. Attached to a helium balloon and equipped with sensors and a video camera, "Camilla" the rubber chicken climbed to 120,000 feet (36,600 m) for science. Her momentous journey was later edited into a video and set to music by the band Chickenfoot.

POP QUIZ!

WHICH OF THE FOLLOWING IS NOT A PRELAUNCH TRADITION FOR RUSSIAN COSMONAUTS?

A. BEING GREETED BY CHEERLEADERS WITH GOLD POM-POMS
B. WATCHING THE ROCKET AS IT IS ROLLED TO THE LAUNCHPAD
C. PLANTING A TREE
D. SPINNING ON SWIVEL CHAIRS

CHECK YOUR ANSWER AT THE BOTTOM OF PAGE 26.

MAKE YOUR OWN FAR-OUT MUSIC VIDEO

1. RECRUIT SOME FUN-LOVING FRIENDS.

2. CHOOSE A FAR-OUT SONG (LEARN THE WORDS IF YOU REALLY WANT TO ROCK IT OUT).

3. FIND A VIDEO CAMERA (A SMARTPHONE WILL DO).

4. PICK A WACKY LOCATION FOR YOUR MUSIC VIDEO, SOMETHING THAT FITS WITH THE SONG'S THEME.

5. ROLL CAMERA.

6. START THE MUSIC AND ...

7. ACTION!

CHAPTER 2

WILD ANIMALS

...NGUTAN PREDICTS SUPER BOWL WINNER · PINK...
...SIDE DOWN IN ICE! · SNOWY OWL VACATIO...
...UTSIDE AGAIN · SQUIRREL SWAPS PICTURES
...EELS THE LOVE · WEIRD ZOO BABIES ROU...
...RMONT · FUNGUS FOIL...

BOOTS LET POOCH PLAY, PAGE 34

ORANGUTAN *PREDICTS* SUPER BOWL WINNER

SALT LAKE CITY, UTAH, U.S.A.

The Seattle Seahawks versus the Denver Broncos: Which football team would win Super Bowl XLVIII? When zookeepers at the Hogle Zoo in Salt Lake City asked Eli the orangutan for his prediction, he didn't hesitate. Eli tore into the enclosure and knocked the papier-mâché Seahawks helmet to the ground, signaling his selection. The team went on to victory, making it the seventh time in a row that Eli correctly predicted the winner of the big game.

SNOWY OWL VACATIONS IN BERMUDA

WHAT ONE SNOWY OWL

WHERE THE ATLANTIC OCEAN ISLAND OF BERMUDA

WHEN NOVEMBER AND DECEMBER 2013

WHY BIOLOGISTS ARE TRYING TO FIGURE OUT WHAT CAUSED THE YOUNG OWL TO TRAVEL SO FAR FROM ITS COLDER, ARCTIC HABITAT. OTHER SNOWY OWLS HAVE BEEN SEEN IN ODD PLACES, AS FAR SOUTH AS TEXAS AND HAWAII, U.S.A. BUT THIS IS THE FIRST TIME A SNOWY OWL WAS REPORTED IN BERMUDA.

NEWS FEED

>>> **HELSINKI, FINLAND:** DUNG BEETLES DIGGING AROUND IN POOP COULD COMBAT GLOBAL WARMING, SCIENTISTS SAY. THE INSECTS' EXCAVATION ALLOWS AIR INTO

PINK DOLPHIN
SPOTTED IN SHIPPING CHANNEL

LAKE CHARLES, LOUISIANA, U.S.A.

What has red eyes, pink skin, and a blowhole? That would be Pinky the albino dolphin. Boaters in the Calcasieu Ship Channel, south of Lake Charles, Louisiana, spotted the dolphin with its pod of normal-colored adults. As an albino, Pinky lacks the pigment that makes most dolphins gray, biologists explain.

SEA CREATURES
LIVE UPSIDE DOWN
IN ICE!

ANEMONES, JUST CHILLIN'

ROSS ICE SHELF, ANTARCTICA

Scientists studying ocean currents along the Antarctic coastline made a shocking discovery: thousands of tiny sea anemones living on the underside of the Ross Ice Shelf. The anemones, each less than 1 inch (2.5 cm) long when contracted, burrow into the underside of the ice and hang upside down. How they maintain their hold in the melting and refreezing ice remains a mystery.

DUNG, WHICH DRIES IT OUT. THIS KILLS MICROBES INSIDE THAT MAKE METHANE, A PLANET-WARMING GAS.

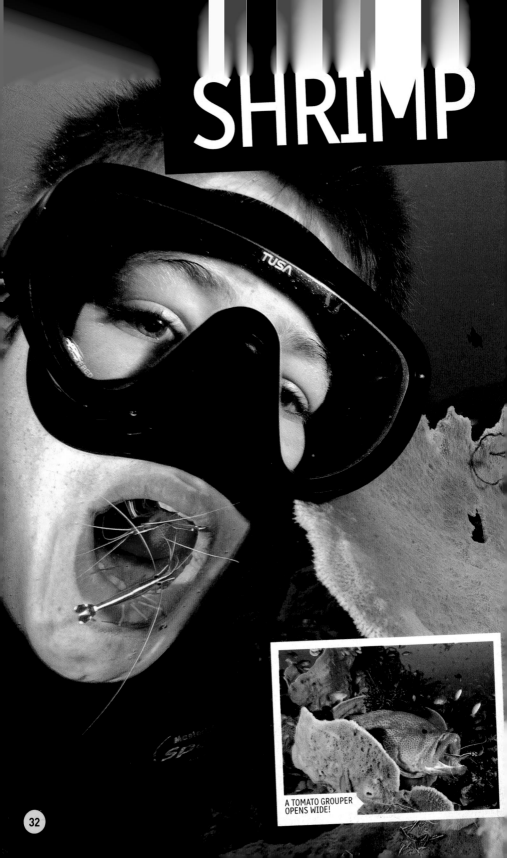

SHRIMP

A TOMATO GROUPER OPENS WIDE!

DENTIST

THE SHRIMPIST WILL SEE YOU NOW

AT SOME **CLEANING STATIONS,** *FISH FORM A LINE* WHILE THEY WAIT FOR *THEIR TURN.*

BALI, INDONESIA

When U.S. teen Russell Laman went diving off the island of Bali, he decided to make like a fish—by having his teeth cleaned tropical reef style!

Russell had noticed tomato groupers and moray eels stopping at this shrimp's "cleaning station" to let the multilegged dentist do its work. So when the station was free, the teen swam up, opened his mouth, and let the shrimp swim right in. "It tickled a little," Russell says of having the shrimp scuttle about inside his mouth, "but not too badly."

He visited other cleaning stations along the reef, including some operated by a type of fish called a cleaner wrasse. But the shrimp was the only cleaner animal brave enough to tackle human teeth. Russell had no trouble letting the shrimp know when he'd had enough. All he had to do was slowly close his mouth, and the shrimp, not wanting to be eaten, shot out to wait on the next customer in line.

BOOTS
LET POOCH PLAY
OUTSIDE
AGAIN

KILGETTY, WALES

Bluey the Weimaraner was so sensitive to the outdoors in the spring and fall that his paws turned red and puffy whenever he went outside. So his owner bought him special Velcro doggie boots. After several stumble-filled weeks of adjustment, his painful paws are now a thing of the past.

ONE UGLY MUG!

UGLY FISH
FEELS THE LOVE

WHO UGLY ANIMAL PRESERVATION SOCIETY

WHAT ADOPTED THE BLOBFISH—VOTED UGLIEST ANIMAL—AS ITS MASCOT

WHERE UNITED KINGDOM

HOW THE UGLY ANIMAL PRESERVATION SOCIETY TEAMED UP WITH THE U.K.'S NATIONAL SCIENCE + ENGINEERING COMPETITION TO HOLD A WORLDWIDE VOTE FOR UGLIEST ANIMAL. THE BLOBFISH SWAM AWAY WITH THE "HONOR."

WHY THE UGLY ANIMAL PRESERVATION SOCIETY WORKS TO BRING ATTENTION TO THE WORLD'S LESS ATTRACTIVE ANIMALS BECAUSE "THE VAST MAJORITY OF LIFE OUT THERE IS DULL AND UGLY."

NEWS FEED

>>> **MOUNT MAUNGANUI BEACH, NEW ZEALAND:** ZORRO THE PIGLET MAY WELL BE THE MOST UNUSUAL (AND YOUNGEST) SURFER TO HIT NEW ZEALAND WAVES.

SQUIRREL SWAPS PICTURES FOR PEANUTS

UNIVERSITY PARK, PENNSYLVANIA, U.S.A.

Since 2012, Penn State student Mary Krupa has used peanuts and patience to lure campus squirrels in for a snack before popping a hat on their heads for a quick pic. The tamest of the bunch, Sneezy, became a worldwide sensation after funny photos of her wearing hats, bunny ears, bows, and even sunglasses appeared online and in newspapers. As fun as this looks, don't try it at home: Squirrels can go nuts on you sometimes!

BIRD STEALS CAMERA, FILMS PENGUINS

SAY CHEESE!

FALKLAND ISLANDS

Filmmakers recording a rockhopper penguin colony got a big surprise when a bird swooped in and stole their camera. Built to look like a rockhopper egg, the camera was snatched by a striated caracara that thought it had scored a snack. Taking to the air, the thief captured aerial footage of the colony before dropping the prize. A pair of vultures then accidentally rolled the camera right back into the colony!

WHEN ZORRO WAS JUST THREE WEEKS OLD, HE BEGAN BALANCING ON THE FRONT OF HIS OWNER'S SURFBOARD!

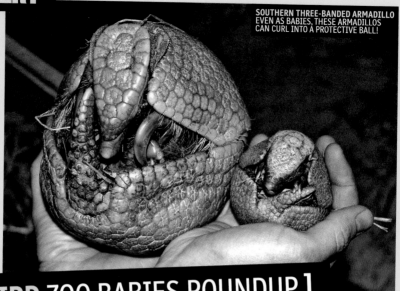

SOUTHERN THREE-BANDED ARMADILLO
EVEN AS BABIES, THESE ARMADILLOS
CAN CURL INTO A PROTECTIVE BALL!

[WEIRD ZOO BABIES ROUNDUP]

Meet the newest adorable oddballs! Their long claws, scaly skin, and enormous ears may prove beauty is in the eye of the beholder!

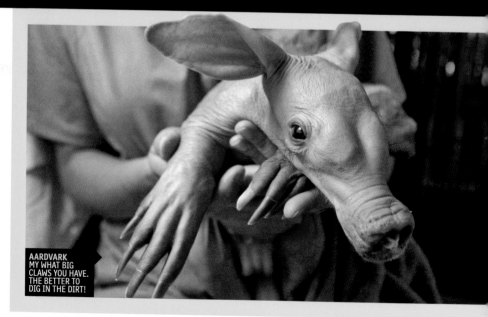

AARDVARK
MY WHAT BIG
CLAWS YOU HAVE.
THE BETTER TO
DIG IN THE DIRT!

IN JUST 15 SECONDS, AN AARDVARK
CAN DIG 2 FEET DEEP.
(0.6 m)

TREE KANGAROO THIS GOODFELLOW'S TREE KANGAROO WAS THE FIRST OF ITS KIND BORN IN A ZOO IN MORE THAN 20 YEARS.

ECHIDNA CALLED A PUGGLE, THIS BABY HATCHED FROM AN EGG INSIDE ITS MOM'S POUCH!

A NEWBORN
ECHIDNA
IS SMALLER
THAN A
JELLY
BEAN.

AYE-AYE LARGE EARS HELP THIS PRIMATE HEAR ITS FAVORITE FOOD: WOOD-DWELLING INSECTS.

TAMANDUA ANTEATER BABY MJ HAS A GRIPPING TAIL THAT HELPS HIM CLING TO TREES.

DOG'S BEST
FRIEND

CARDIFF, WALES

SOMETIMES EVEN A DOG NEEDS A GUIDE DOG.
Eddie the black Lab and Milo, a terrier mix, were
already buddies when Eddie went blind. He began
running into people, trees, benches, and other
objects that stood in his way. And even though Eddie
could hear his owner calling him, he couldn't always
find his way back. So Milo started lending a helping
paw, wearing bells on his collar so Eddie could follow
along and play fetch. Their owner even connects
them with a leash, so Milo can take Eddie for a walk.

ZOMBIES ATTACK!

PARASITE DRAWS RATS TO CATS!

STANFORD, CALIFORNIA, U.S.A.

When a rat smells a cat, it turns tail and flees—unless it's been infected with *Toxoplasma gondii*. This single-cell parasite reproduces inside of cats, and what better way to move from cat to cat than by hitching a ride inside a rat? Stanford University scientists recently discovered that the parasite makes its way into the rat's brain, where it overrides the rodent's desire to run and hide when it gets a whiff of cat. Not only that—the mind-controlled, now love-struck rat actually seeks out cats!

RATS' FRONT TEETH CAN GROW 5.5 INCHES A YEAR. (14 cm)

NEWS FEED

>>> **COSTA RICA:** VAMPIRE WASPS IN COSTA RICA TURN SPIDERS INTO ZOMBIES. WASP LARVAE CLING TO ORB-WEAVER SPIDERS, DRINKING THEIR BLOOD.

A BEEHIVE CAN MAKE **2 POUNDS** (1 kg) OF HONEY A DAY.

"ZOMBIE BEES" INVADE VERMONT

VERMONT, U.S.A.

Beekeepers in Vermont have reported some strange sights at night: honeybees wandering in circles, their movements jerky and uncoordinated—in other words, zombie-like! Inside these "zombie bees" live the larvae, or young, of a parasitic fly. They eat the innards of the bees, making them act oddly (putting a creepy twist on the idea of zombies eating brains). The flies are the latest in a long list of problems affecting U.S. honeybees and contributing to colony collapse disorder—the mysterious disappearance of entire bee colonies.

FOR **EVERY PERSON** ON EARTH THERE ARE AN ESTIMATED **1.5 MILLION ANTS.**

FUNGUS FOILS ANT BRAINS

THAILAND

Ants typically stick close to their nests, except to wander along well-defined scent trails in search of food. Unless they're infected with zombie fungus, that is. The fungus controls the insects' behavior, causing them to clamber up and clamp their jaws onto a leaf growing above where they usually forage. The infected ants maintain their grip after they die a short time later. Then the fungus grows out of their bodies and releases spores that fall to the ground to zombify even more insects.

AFTER ONE TO TWO WEEKS, THE LARVAE HAVE THE SPIDERS WEAVING TAILOR-MADE COCOONS THAT THE YOUNG WASPS USE TO GROW INTO ADULTS.

GATOR GETS NEW TAIL

MR. STUBBS SWIMS AGAIN!

STUBBS SHOWS OFF HIS STUMP.

STUBBS'S NEW TAIL STRAPS AROUND HIS HIND LEGS.

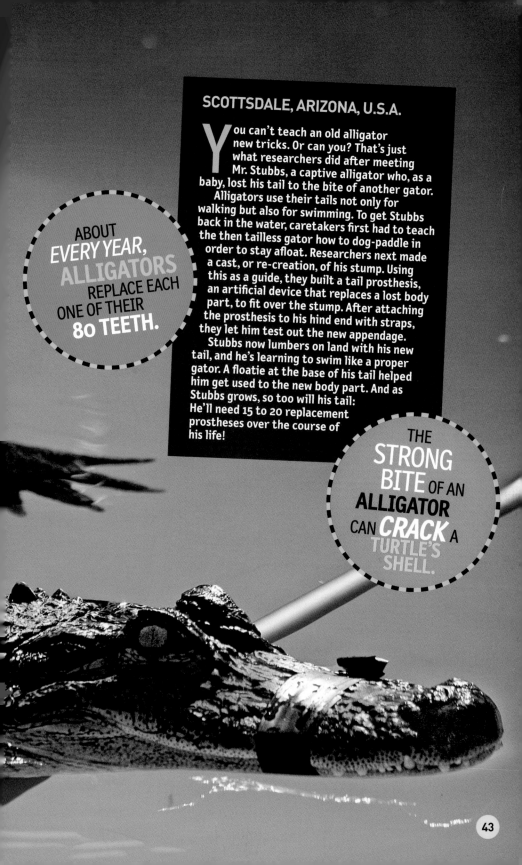

SCOTTSDALE, ARIZONA, U.S.A.

You can't teach an old alligator new tricks. Or can you? That's just what researchers did after meeting Mr. Stubbs, a captive alligator who, as a baby, lost his tail to the bite of another gator. Alligators use their tails not only for walking but also for swimming. To get Stubbs back in the water, caretakers first had to teach the then tailless gator how to dog-paddle in order to stay afloat. Researchers next made a cast, or re-creation, of his stump. Using this as a guide, they built a tail prosthesis, an artificial device that replaces a lost body part, to fit over the stump. After attaching the prosthesis to his hind end with straps, they let him test out the new appendage.

Stubbs now lumbers on land with his new tail, and he's learning to swim like a proper gator. A floatie at the base of his tail helped him get used to the new body part. And as Stubbs grows, so too will his tail: He'll need 15 to 20 replacement prostheses over the course of his life!

ABOUT EVERY YEAR, ALLIGATORS REPLACE EACH ONE OF THEIR 80 TEETH.

THE STRONG BITE OF AN ALLIGATOR CAN CRACK A TURTLE'S SHELL.

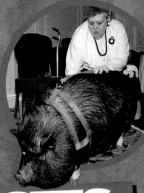

DOG SAVES SOLDIERS

PIG GETS HELP FOR HER OWNER

1943

In World War II, a shepherd mix named Chips became the first dog to be awarded a Silver Star for bravery. Chips ran for help when his platoon was trapped by enemy fire. He also alerted soldiers that enemy troops were approaching and attacked them. Despite his bravery, Chips didn't get to keep his medal: The military later decided medals were for people only.

1998

When Jo Ann Altsman took in a potbellied pig, she didn't expect a savior. But that's what the Pennsylvania, U.S.A., woman got. Altsman suffered a heart attack while home alone with her pet pig, LuLu. The clever pig forced her way through the dog door, pushed open the gate, and threw herself onto the street. When a man headed to the house to let Altsman know her pig was in distress, he found the woman in need of help.

>>> AMAZING ANIMALS TO THE RESCUE

1986

A boy made international news after he fell into a gorilla enclosure in a zoo in Jersey, England, and seemed to be protected by one of the apes. A silverback male, Jambo, sat next to the boy and kept other gorillas away. Jambo even put a hand on the human, as if to comfort him, while rescuers figured out how to get the boy out. Thanks to Jambo, the boy made a full recovery.

GORILLA STANDS GUARD OVER INJURED BOY

ELEPHANT SAVES GIRL FROM TSUNAMI

2004

When an earthquake in the Indian Ocean sent a massive tsunami sweeping across Thai beaches, Ningnong the elephant ran for the hills—with an eight-year-old girl onboard. Whether the elephant ran because it noticed the water receding (as it does before crashing ashore in a tsunami) or because its owner instructed it to remains unclear. Regardless of the reason, Ningnong saved the girl from a deadly wall of water that day.

BELUGA WHALE RESCUES DIVER

2009

Participating in a contest, Yang Yun sank to the bottom of a water tank at Polar Land, an aquarium in China. There she planned to stay as long as she could. But when she tried to return to the surface as her air was running out, she found her legs paralyzed by the frigid water. Mila, a beluga whale that lives in the tank, noticed Yun's distress. Gripping the woman's leg in her mouth, the whale pushed Yun to the surface, saving her life.

ANIMAL SMARTS
IN THE NEWS

See if you can guess how these animals used their heads to make headlines! Find the correct answers in the key at the bottom of page 47.

1.

1. IN 2012, SCIENTISTS REPORTED THAT A CHIMPANZEE AT A SWEDISH ZOO:

A. USED AN APPLE TO DISTRACT VISITORS BEFORE THROWING STASHED ROCKS AT THEM.

B. PEELED A DOZEN APPLES AND BAKED A PIE.

C. JUGGLED APPLES ONE-HANDED WHILE SWINGING.

2.

2. IN 2014, SCIENTISTS RECORDED A WILD CROW IN NEW CALEDONIA:

A. USING A BLADE OF GRASS AS A MUSICAL INSTRUMENT.

B. COMPLETING AN EIGHT-STEP PUZZLE IN ORDER TO REACH FOOD.

C. USING STICKS TO DRILL HOLES FOR DECORATION.

3. IN 2014, STAFF AT A NEW ZEALAND AQUARIUM REPORTED THAT AN OCTOPUS:

A. OPENED A JAR IN LESS THAN 60 SECONDS.

B. CHANGED ITS COLORS TO MATCH A PLAID BACKGROUND.

C. PULLED OPEN A LOCKED TREASURE CHEST.

3.

4.

4. IN 2011, A PHOTOGRAPHER IN LONDON'S RICHMOND PARK CAUGHT THIS STAG:

A. SHOWING OFF A NEW HAIRDO.

B. PLAYING BLINDMAN'S BLUFF WITH THE OTHER DEER.

C. ROLLING IN MOSS AS HE TRIED TO ATTRACT FEMALES.

CHAPTER 3

INCREDIBLE
INVENTIONS

MICKING MOTHER NATURE • SCIENTISTS C
POUNDS • BUILDING MAKES FACES! • MII
OW-IN-THE-DARK ROADS • DOGS GET FI
TEBOARDERS CATCH AIR ON WATER • IN!
MOUSE IN YOUR

SQUIRRELS
HORSE AROUND,
PAGE 67

TAPE HOLDS HUNDRE
ING A BREEZE! • REAL-LI
WATER OUT OF THIN AIR
LIVES • PEN MAKES ART IN T
MIMICKING MOTHER NATUR
DREDS OF POUNDS • BUILDING MAK
REAL-LIFE GLOW-IN-THE-DARK
WATERBOARDERS CATCH AIR

MIMICKING
MOTHER NATURE

CAMERA BUGS OUT!

URBANA, ILLINOIS, U.S.A.

Scientists at the University of Illinois at Urbana-Champaign developed a camera that can produce pictures similar to what an insect eye sees. The half-inch (1.2-cm)-diameter dome is covered with 180 tiny bump-like lenses (about as many lenses as in the eye of a fire ant). Each focuses light onto a miniscule structure that converts light energy into electrical signals. Those signals combine to create a wide-angle image. The scientists say adding even more lenses would allow the cam to take panoramic pictures that are just as sharp as those snapped by digital cameras.

BEES SEE **COLORS** *FASTER* THAN ANY OTHER **ANIMAL.**

NEWS FEED

>>> BERKELEY, CALIFORNIA, U.S.A.: ROBOTS OF THE FUTURE MAY FIND THEIR WAY AROUND WITH CATLIKE WHISKERS. THE FLEXIBLE STRUCTURES ARE SENSITIVE

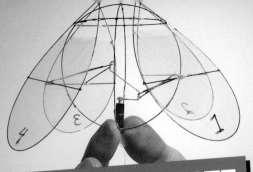

SCIENTISTS CREATE FLYING JELLYFISH

NEW YORK, NEW YORK, U.S.A.

When scientists at New York University set out to build a machine that could hover, they weren't thinking about jellyfish. But that's what the flying device they designed looks like. After watching how shapes like pyramids and cones float in the air (and how an umbrella works), they were inspired to build a winged machine with a similar shape. After many adjustments, they figured out how to get their four-inch (10-cm) machine to hover safely: by flapping its wings out of sync. They then noticed that the machine's movement resembles how a jellyfish swims through the sea.

LION'S MANE JELLYFISH CAN BE AS BIG AS *8 FEET* (2.4 m) **ACROSS.**

GECKOS CAN REGROW LOST TAILS.

GECKO-INSPIRED TAPE HOLDS HUNDREDS OF POUNDS

AMHERST, MASSACHUSETTS, U.S.A.

Want to hang a 700-pound (317-kg) picture on a wall? Just tape it up! A new type of tape inspired by the stiff connection between a gecko's tendons and skin helps a picture stick to a wall much like the animal does. Designed by scientists at the University of Massachusetts Amherst, Geckskin simply needs to be pressed against a smooth surface, just like ordinary tape. A piece the size of an index card can support that heavy picture. And a simple twist pulls it off the wall, leaving no sticky residue behind.

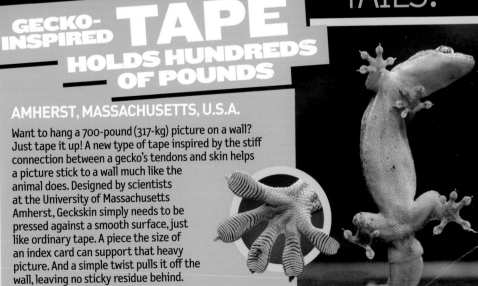

ENOUGH TO DETECT SOMETHING AS SLIGHT AS A DOLLAR BILL. THE "E-WHISKERS" WOULD COME IN HANDY FOR SQUEEZING THROUGH TIGHT SPACES.

THE AMAZING
SPIDER-BOY!

WHEN TEACHERS SAY THEIR STUDENTS ARE CLIMBING THE WALLS, THEY DON'T MEAN IT LITERALLY. Except when that student is Hibiki Kono. The teen used two inexpensive vacuum cleaners to create a wall-climbing device for his design and technology class. He crafted two squares with special seals around the edges and handles to hold on to, then he attached each to a vacuum hose. With a flip of a switch, the squares used the vacuums' suction to stick to the wall. The device was strong enough to support Hibiki and his teacher, who hung from the ceiling!

BUILDING
MAKES **FACES!**

AMAZING ARCHITECTURE
AT THE OLYMPICS

МегаФон

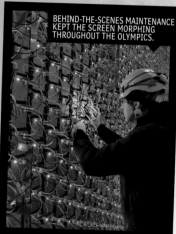

BEHIND-THE-SCENES MAINTENANCE KEPT THE SCREEN MORPHING THROUGHOUT THE OLYMPICS.

SOCHI, RUSSIA

Athletes' faces weren't the only mugs on display at the Sochi Olympics in 2014. One side of the MegaFon building in Olympic Park morphed into massive 3-D faces made from scans of people who posed in special photo booths inside.

Called "MegaFaces," the Mount Rushmore—like display was designed by Asif Khan and worked much like a pin screen does. Eleven thousand LED-tipped, pinlike structures pushed outward from the building to create 26-foot (8-m)-high renderings of visitors' faces.

Khan says he was inspired in part by the popularity of posting pictures online and sharing selfies. The exhibit, he says, allowed everyone to be the face of the Olympics and turned the "everyday moment into something epic."

MINI-WINDMILLS
MAKE CELL PHONE CHARGING A BREEZE

ARLINGTON, TEXAS, U.S.A.

Supersmall windmills could one day be used to charge mobile devices such as cell phones. Developed by Smitha Rao and J.-C. Chiao at the University of Texas at Arlington, the tiny turbines would coat a special charging sleeve. By slipping the sleeve on a phone and holding it up in a breeze or waving it around, users could recharge anywhere.

A PENNY!

UN PANEL QUE PRODUCE
AGUA POTABLE DEL AIRE
ES INGENIO EN ACCIÓN.

EXAMEN DE ADMISIÓN
5 DE MARZO

UTEC

BILLBOARD
CREATES WATER
OUT OF THIN AIR

WHAT A GIANT BILLBOARD THAT TURNS HUMID AIR INTO DRINKING WATER

WHERE LIMA, PERU

HOW AIR IS FILTERED AND THEN RUN THROUGH CONDENSERS THAT DRAW THE WATER FROM IT (THINK OF HOW WATER COLLECTS ON A COLD GLASS ON A HUMID DAY). THAT WATER IS THEN PURIFIED AND STORED IN A TANK AT THE BILLBOARD'S BASE. A FAUCET LETS THIRSTY PASSERSBY TAKE A DRINK.

WHY THE UNIVERSITY OF ENGINEERING AND TECHNOLOGY OF PERU WANTED TO SHOW HOW CREATIVITY CAN HELP SOLVE PROBLEMS. LIMA TYPICALLY RECEIVES ONLY HALF AN INCH (1.25 CM) OF RAIN EACH YEAR. BUT ITS LOCATION NEAR THE PACIFIC COAST MEANS THE AIR IS SATURATED WITH WATER. THE BILLBOARD GIVES PERUVIANS ACCESS TO THAT AIRBORNE WATER, CREATING NEARLY 26 GALLONS (100 L) OF DRINKING WATER EACH DAY.

NEWS FEED

>>> **SAN FRANCISCO, CALIFORNIA, U.S.A.:** EVER WISHED YOUR PANTS COULD DOUBLE AS DRUMS? YOUR DREAMS HAVE COME TRUE. DRUMPANTS,

REAL-LIFE GLOW-IN-THE-DARK ROADS

OSS, THE NETHERLANDS

Long, dark nights don't necessarily mean dangerous driving when the road glows neon green. A single stretch of road in the Netherlands has been striped with special paint that charges in sunlight, then glows for up to eight hours at night. So far, the paint has been used only in that area to test how well it withstands wear and tear.

DOGS GET *FETCH-ING* GRINS

VARIOUS LOCATIONS

Chasing balls makes dogs happy, but chasing Grinz balls makes dogs smile, too. The toothy toy has a big grin on one side and a hole to fill the toy with treats on the other, increasing the odds that Fido will snatch it up with a smile.

INVENTED BY MUSICIAN TYLER FREEMAN, HAVE SENSORS THAT VELCRO ONTO THE BODY—OVER OR UNDER CLOTHING—TO LET USERS TAP OUT MORE THAN 100 DIFFERENT SOUNDS.

WINGED WATERCRAFT

Italian aircraft builders developed this flying boat to cross the Atlantic. The massive structure boasted nine wings (three sets of three), eight engines, and two pontoons for stability. During its test flight, the Noviplano took off from Italy's Lake Maggiore and flew 60 feet (18 m) high before crashing. The pilot emerged wet but unharmed. The plane never did cross the ocean—it never even made it past the lake!

1921

PERSONAL HELICOPTER

George Sablier of Saint-Étienne, France, invented this one-person helicopter. Worn like a backpack, the 60-pound (27-kg) whirlybird boasted a six-horsepower engine. Sablier claimed it could fly at a speed of 31 miles an hour (50 km/h) for up to ten hours. Whether it actually flew—and whether it did so without spinning the wearer around like a top—remains unclear. Skeptics say the craft as shown in the photo never could have actually flown.

1954

>>> HIGH-FLYING IDEAS

1947

FLYING CAR

Why drive when you can fly? And why pick one when you can have both? Theodore Hall designed this plane/car hybrid with removable wings and tail so the vehicle could easily transition from sky to ground. Hall built two models. The first, shown here, crashed due to lack of fuel. The second model flew, but the idea never really got off the ground.

THE MOST **POWERFUL** JET **ENGINE** HAS MORE OOMPH THAN THE **TITANIC** AND A **SPACE ROCKET** COMBINED!

BLOW-UP AIRPLANE

1956

Goodyear may be known for blimps, but it's also branched out into airplanes—inflatable ones, that is. Intended for wartime, the deflated planes plus their engines could be air-dropped to troops in need of transport. The planes could be inflated with a bicycle pump in a mere five minutes. The motor continually pumped air into the inner-tube-like body to prevent it from deflating during flight.

THE X-WING

1986

What do you get when you cross a helicopter with an airplane? The X-Wing. Engineers created the X-Wing to get the best of both types of aircraft: the vertical lift of a helicopter and the fast forward motion of an airplane. Intended for use in search-and-rescue operations, the X-Wing wasn't able to save itself. Despite a series of successful test flights, the program ended after only a few of the aircraft were produced.

PEN MAKES ART IN THE AIR

BOSTON, MASSACHUSETTS, U.S.A.

Tired of sketching on paper? Try drawing in the air! Inventors created the 3Doodler, a pen that draws with plastic instead of ink and can be used to make 3-D structures—just draw up or down! The pen plugs in and warms up, melting the plastic and letting creativity flow.

KEYBOARD PANTS
PUT A MOUSE IN YOUR
POCKET

WHO ERIK DE NIJS

WHAT CREATED BEAUTY AND THE GEEK PANTS WITH A BUILT-IN COMPUTER KEYBOARD

WHERE UTRECHT, THE NETHERLANDS

HOW A KEYBOARD IS BUILT INTO JEANS, RIGHT ACROSS THE LAP. THE MOUSE—TETHERED TO THE RIGHT HIP—SLIPS INTO A SPECIALLY DESIGNED BACK POCKET WHEN NOT IN USE. SMALL SPEAKERS LOCATED ON THE OUTER KNEES PROVIDE SOUND. THE JEANS CONNECT TO A COMPUTER USING BLUETOOTH WIRELESS TECHNOLOGY OR VIA A CABLE THAT CAN DOUBLE AS A BELT.

OUTCOME NIJS WANTED TO COMBINE THE WORLDS OF FASHION AND TECHNOLOGY—BECAUSE GEEK CAN BE CHIC.

NEWS FEED

>>> WALTHAM, MASSACHUSETTS, U.S.A.: WHAT LEAPS SMALL BUILDINGS IN A SINGLE BOUND, BESIDES SUPERMAN? SAND FLEA! THIS 11-POUND (5-KG)

INVISIBLE BIKE HELMET
SAVES HAIRDOS, LIVES

MALMÖ, SWEDEN

Two Swedish designers noticed that though bike helmets can save lives, many people don't wear them. So they stopped riders to ask why. The most common answer: Helmets would mess up their hair. So the designers invented the Hövding air bag helmet. Worn as a collar, the air bag deploys around the sides, back, and top of the head only when the rider suddenly changes position, such as during a crash.

SKATEBOARDERS CATCH AIR ON WATER

BOARDS GO OVERBOARD

LAKE TAHOE, CALIFORNIA, U.S.A.

You've heard of waterskiing, but what about water skateboarding? Designers Jeff King and Jerry Blohm created this 36-foot (11-m) floating skateboard ramp. Made of stained and polished wood, the 7,300-pound (3,311-kg) ramp sits on a floating platform in Lake Tahoe. Professional skateboarder Bob Burnquist gave it a trial run, launching himself right into the water for his finale.

WHEELED ROBOT JUMPS 30 FEET (9 M) INTO THE AIR, HIGH ENOUGH TO LAND ON ROOFTOPS, SKIP STAIRS, OR EVEN POP THROUGH A SECOND-STORY WINDOW.

DOGGLES

TO THE RESCUE!

TIVIDALE, ENGLAND

THIS DOG'S NOT TOO COOL FOR SCHOOL—his eyes are just too sensitive for the sun. In 2013, Bugsy the mixed-breed pooch went out for a sunny afternoon walk for the first time in four years, thanks to his new Doggles. The eyewear blocks the sun's ultraviolet rays, which cause Bugsy's eyes to turn red and watery. Before he got his Doggles, Bugsy went for walks only in the early morning and evening, when the sun was low in the sky. Now he can set out in style any time of day.

CARDBOARD BIKE
VARNISHED
CARDBOARD AND
RECYCLED CAR
TIRES MAKE FOR A
LOW-COST RIDE.

[**WEIRD** WHEELED INVENTIONS]

These inventors didn't reinvent the wheel—they just did really weird things with it!

THE
CARDBOARD
BIKE IS
WATERPROOF,
FIREPROOF,
AND CAN
SUPPORT UP TO
300
POUNDS.
(136 kg)

FISH ON WHEELS
NEED TO "WALK" YOUR
FISH? A CAMERA ATOP
THIS TANK HELPS IT
MOVE IN THE DIRECTION
THE FISH SWIMS.

BICYCLE ELEVATOR
FORGET FORWARD MOTION. PEDALING THIS BIKE LIFTS YOU STRAIGHT UP TO A TREE HOUSE!

RYNO
THIS ONE-WHEELED WONDER REQUIRES RIDERS TO BALANCE ONLY FROM SIDE TO SIDE.

WATER BIKES
CAN TRAVEL AS FAST AS
10 MILES (16 km/h)
AN HOUR.

WATER BIKE
EMPTY WATER BOTTLES AND A MODIFIED WHEEL MAKE FOR EASY BIKE TRAVEL—ON WATER!

GUESS THE INVENTION

Can you figure out the purpose of these unusual inventions? Choose your answer, then check the key at the bottom of the page.

1. THIS CHAIR IS:

A. ROCKING THE NEW TREND OF SWEATERS FOR FURNITURE

B. WHAT SCIENTISTS WORKING IN ANTARCTICA SIT ON

C. WRAPPED WITH A WOOLEN BLANKET FOR SITTERS TO SNUGGLE UNDER

2. THIS FURRY ROBOT:

A. DUSTS THE UNDERSIDE OF FURNITURE

B. CHASES MICE

C. PURRS LIKE A CAT WHEN YOU PET IT

GUESS THE INVENTION ANSWERS: 1) C; 2) C; 3) A; 4) B
REAL OR FAKE ANSWERS: THEY'RE ALL REAL—YOU CAN'T MAKE THIS STUFF UP!

3. THESE PANTS PROVIDE WEARERS:

A. A HANDY PLACE TO HAVE A PICNIC

B. THE LATEST, LOW-HANGING FASHION STATEMENT

C. LIMITED MOBILITY TO LESSEN THE LENGTH OF THEIR STRIDE; WALKING WITH SMALL STEPS IS "IN"

REAL OR FAKE?

WHICH OF THESE WACKY CREATIONS ARE REAL-LIFE INVENTIONS?

A. UNDERWEAR THAT PREVENTS THE SCENT OF A TOOT FROM ESCAPING

B. AN ALARM CLOCK THAT WAKES YOU WITH THE SCENT OF A FRESHLY COOKED STRIP OF BACON

C. BOOTIES WITH SPONGES ON THE BOTTOM FOR STAND-UP FLOOR SCRUBBING

D. A HOODIE FOR TWO

4. THIS HORSE'S HEAD IS:

A. A HALLOWEEN COSTUME FOR SQUIRRELS

B. A SQUIRREL FEEDER

C. A DISGUISE THAT KEEPS SQUIRRELS SAFE FROM DOGS AND CATS

CHAPTER 4

FREAKY
FOOD

BLACK HOT DOGS, PAGE 80

THIS RESTAURANT REQUIRES A PYTHON? • HOT SAUCE CAUSES SPICY STINK • BIG APPETITES • LUNCH BOX DELIVERY • THIS LUNCH HEATS ITSELF

ALS? JUST PRESS PRINT! • ANCIENT MUMMI
E SALES • HAVE A HOOT AT OWL CAFES • PEPPER
OT DOGS! • FREAKY FRUITS AND VEGGIES • LIT
AN A SPEEDING ... SANDWICH? • WORLD'S LARG
ALONG WITH YOUR SANDWICH • HOT HOT HO
M • VERY ODD VENDING MACHINES • THE SIST
OR • OR JUST REALLY GROSS? • JUST PRESS PR

SHHH!
THIS RESTAURANT REQUIRES SILENCE

NO LAUGHING, NO SNIFFLING, NO CHITCHAT!

BROOKLYN, NEW YORK, U.S.A.

It's one thing to not talk with your mouth full, but not talking at all? One Brooklyn restaurant hosts special "silent meals," where diners must keep themselves—and their cell phones—quiet for the entire four-course dinner. The owner reportedly based the idea on the noiseless breakfasts he experienced at a Buddhist monastery, which encouraged more focus on the food.

RECORD-SETTING GIRL SCOUT COOKIE SALES

WHO KATIE FRANCIS

WHAT SOLD 21,477 BOXES OF GIRL SCOUT COOKIES, BREAKING THE ORGANIZATION'S NATIONAL RECORD

WHERE OKLAHOMA CITY, OKLAHOMA, U.S.A.

WHEN SPRING 2014

HOW TO BEAT THE SCOUTS' PREVIOUS COOKIE SALES RECORD, SET IN THE 1980S, KATIE SPENT ABOUT SEVEN HOURS SELLING EACH WEEKDAY (AND STILL MANAGED TO FIT IN SCHOOL!). ON SATURDAYS AND SUNDAYS, SHE PULLED 11- TO 13-HOUR DAYS! SHE ASKED EVERYONE SHE SAW, AND THIN MINTS WERE HER BEST SELLERS.

NEWS FEED

>>> **TOKYO, JAPAN:** THE WORLD'S FIRST KIT KAT–ONLY SHOP OPENED IN TOKYO IN JANUARY 2014. THERE YOU CAN TRY SOME OF THE WACKY

INSTA-MEALS? *JUST PRESS* PRINT!

BARCELONA, SPAIN

Forget the microwave. The Foodini 3-D printer may be your new favorite kitchen gadget. The machine quickly turns fresh ingredients into complete dishes. Perhaps the best part: Your favorite foods—nuggets, tiny quiches, crackers, chocolates—can be printed in fun shapes such as animals and snowmen.

ANCIENT MUMMIES BURIED WITH CHEESE

CHEESE

CHEESE

TAKLIMAKAN DESERT, CHINA

Scientists have discovered the world's oldest cheese, which was buried with 3,600-year-old mummies in the Taklimakan Desert. The ancient dairy product wasn't made like a hard cheese like cheddar. Rather, it was made the same way as today's kefir, a sour beverage and cheese. And it likely wasn't intended to be eaten thousands of years later—not that you'd want to eat it, anyway!

Nestlé
KitKat
宇治抹茶

FLAVORS FOUND ONLY IN JAPAN: PURPLE POTATO, CINNAMON COOKIE, WASABI, GREEN TEA, AND EVEN EUROPEAN CHEESE!

LUNCH **BOX** DELIVERY

1890

In India, people often eat lunch out of cylindrical, stacking tins called tiffins. Around 1890, a service was started to deliver homemade lunches packed in these tins to people at work—a sort of early pizza delivery person. The service is still used in India today, and the *dabbawalas*, or tiffin deliverers, are known for always being on time.

SOME
200,000
TIFFINS ARE
DELIVERED TO
OFFICES IN
MUMBAI, INDIA,
DAILY.

>>> THINKING OUTSIDE THE (LUNCH) BOX

1954

FASTER THAN A SPEEDING ... SANDWICH?

The first lunch box to feature Superman appeared in 1954, and boy, was it popular. It depicted the caped super-hero battling a golden robot. Today the lunch box is considered a valuable collectible. A few have been sold at auction for well over $10,000 each!

WORLD'S LARGEST LUNCH BOX MUSEUM

1991

Perhaps Allen Woodall is holding on to so many lunch boxes in the hopes that one will be worth as much as that Superman pail. Woodall has more than 2,000 lunch boxes and thermoses on display at his Lunch Box Museum in Columbus, Georgia, U.S.A. The collection includes TV show personalities, popular cartoon characters, and the 1950s cowboy-themed lunch boxes that were among the first decorated pails.

SING ALONG WITH YOUR SANDWICH

2012

It's a lunch box ... it's a music box ... it's a musical lunch box! In 2012, a Portuguese company started selling Soundwiches: sandwiches like ham and cheese, smoked salmon, and turkey served in a metal lunch box (that you later return) that plays a song when you open it. Each sells for less than $10, meaning you pay only a small fee for lunch and a song!

2009

GOURMET **MEALS** SERVED IN 18-KARAT-GOLD **BENTO BOXES** SOLD FOR **$229,000** IN A **JAPANESE** DEPARTMENT STORE.

THIS LUNCH HEATS ITSELF!

Peanut butter and jelly is a great lunch. But the Mo:Ben self-heating lunch box was designed for days when you want to pack macaroni and cheese, spaghetti and meatballs, soup, or any other hot meal. To warm its contents, the stylish orange-and-white container would simply need to be plugged into a wall outlet.

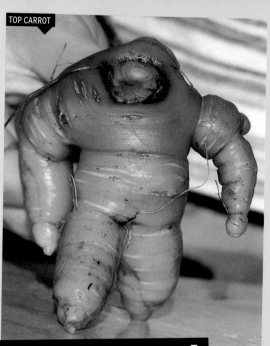

TOP CARROT

TOMAT-OH!

[FREAKY FRUITS AND VEGGIES]

Attention gardeners: Be sure to pay attention to the produce you're picking. Otherwise, you may miss the creative creatures growing right under your nose! See if you can spot some funny figures for yourself. *Mmm ... weird and delicious!*

FACE PLANT

STRAW-BEARY

STRAWBERRIES ARE MEMBERS OF THE ROSE FAMILY.

TEDDY TATER

AN **BRITISH MAN** ONCE **GREW** AN **11**-POUND POTATO. (5-kg)

SOME BUNNY

SHOW OF HANDS

DUCK, DUCK, CUCUMBER!?

LITTLE PEOPLE,

SEATTLE, WASHINGTON, U.S.A.

Can you imagine getting paid to play with your food? Christopher Boffoli can—he's a Seattle-based writer, filmmaker, and photographer who's best known for the hundreds of playful scenes he has created using regular food items as playthings for teeny-tiny toy people. A book of his funniest pictures, *Big Appetites*, was published in 2013. Boffoli says he loves his subject matter because "no matter what country you live in or what language you speak, everyone plays with toys and we all eat food." Here he answers a few questions about his awesome job.

Have you always played with your food?
I never really played with my food when I was a kid. I enjoyed mealtime way too much.

What's the weirdest food you've worked with? Did you try it?
I am very adventurous when it comes to food, and there is not much I dislike (though I definitely think black licorice is disgusting). I have traveled extensively around the world and eaten things like fried crickets, kangaroo, sea urchin, alligator, krill, and llama, just to name a few. So by comparison, the food that I have used in my work is fairly tame. Perhaps some of the more unusual subjects of my work have been things like octopus, Romanesco broccoli, and Washington State freshwater crayfish. I'm willing to try any food, with the exception of black licorice of course.

BIG APPETITES

THIS PHOTOGRAPHER ENCOURAGES EVERYONE TO PLAY WITH THEIR FOOD

"PAPAYA GOLFING"

"RAMEN PERCH"

ARCHITECTS HAVE STUDIED **ROMANESCO BROCCOLI'S SHAPE** *AS INSPIRATION* FOR **NEW BUILDINGS.**

THE SISTINE CHAPEL
IN SPRINKLES

LONDON, ENGLAND

WHO'S HUNGRY FOR A HISTORY LESSON? To celebrate the 450th anniversary of the death of Italian artist Michelangelo, baker Michelle Wibowo re-created his famous "Creation of Adam" fresco from the ceiling of the Sistine Chapel— entirely out of cake decorations! Wibowo spent 168 hours placing each edible item by hand to form the full-size replica. The decorations include some 10,000 marshmallows and about half a billion sprinkles in 24 colors. To hold it all together, the baker used butter, powdered sugar, and vanilla frosting as "glue." This masterpiece is now a meal, too!

HAVE A HOOT AT OWL CAFÉS

OWL TAKE YOUR ORDER, PLEASE.

TOKYO, JAPAN

What's better than a cup of tea? A cup of tea with an adorable, wide-eyed owl friend! Japan—already home to cat, bunny, and goat cafés—now has coffee and tea shops in Tokyo and Osaka that showcase owls, both on display and to interact with. Some even serve supercute owl-themed snacks to enjoy while you bird-watch.

BLACK HOT DOGS!

WHAT THE BLACK TERRA HOT DOG, 12 INCHES (30 CM) OF COAL-COLORED SAUSAGE AND BUN

WHERE VEGAS PREMIUM HOT DOG IN THE AKIHABARA DISTRICT OF TOKYO, JAPAN

WHEN PREMIERED IN EARLY 2013

HOW AN EDIBLE DYE MADE FROM GROUND-UP, BURNED BAMBOO GIVES THE FAST FOOD ITS COLOR. REPORTEDLY, THE DARK DYE DOESN'T CHANGE THE TASTE OF THE HOT DOG. YOU CAN HAVE IT TOPPED WITH ALL THE USUAL CHOICES: KETCHUP, MUSTARD, ONIONS, WHATEVER.

WHY HAMBURGERS WITH BLACK BUNS HAVE SHOWN UP ON FAST FOOD MENUS AROUND ASIA (EVEN AT BURGER KING), SO IT ONLY MAKES SENSE THAT HOT DOGS WERE NEXT. VEGAS PREMIUM HOT DOG REPORTS THE BLACK DOG IS ONE OF ITS MOST POPULAR MENU ITEMS.

NEWS FEED

››› **SEATTLE, WASHINGTON, U.S.A.:** "FOR WHEN YOU SWEAT LIKE A PIG" IS THE TAGLINE OF A NEW BACON-SCENTED DEODORANT PRODUCED BY

PEPPERONI OR PYTHON?

FORT MYERS, FLORIDA, U.S.A.

So many pythons now call the Everglades home that Floridians aren't sure what to do with the supersize snakes. Evan's Neighborhood Pizza has an idea: Put them on a crust and top them with cheese! The restaurant's Everglades pizza features fresh python meat, frog legs, and alligator sausage. The shop sells about five of the pies per week, sometimes more.

SNAKES ON A PIZZA!

HOT SAUCE CAUSES SPICY STINK

IRWINDALE, CALIFORNIA, U.S.A.

Residents of a Southern California neighborhood complained in late 2013 that the local Sriracha hot sauce factory was polluting the area with its peppery scent. People claimed production of the popular condiment, nicknamed "The Rooster," was causing them to cough and tear up. The company disputed the claims but installed new ventilation systems anyway and opened its factory to public tours.

J&D'S FOODS, MAKER OF MANY BACON-THEMED ITEMS. DON'T WEAR DEODORANT? NO PROBLEM. THEY ALSO MAKE SUNSCREEN.

HOT, HOT, HOT!

PIZZA SO SPICY IT'LL MAKE YOU SEE STARS

SLEAFORD, ENGLAND

The "Death by Pizza" challenge is totally real and totally lethal to your taste buds. The Little Italy Pizza Co., a pizzeria a few hours north of London, created what it's calling the world's hottest pizza. It's so spicy that owner James Broderick says most people have hiccups after about 30 seconds, many experience numbness, and a few have even hallucinated or vomited.

The potentially dangerous pie is topped with cheese and a sauce that, thanks to a mix of superspicy chilies, is as hot as pepper spray! (Some of the sauce's chilies are even hotter, but mixing in herbs, tomatoes, and onions lowers its heat.) If anyone finishes the 12-inch (30-cm) pizza in 30 minutes or less, he or she wins prize money that more than covers the cost of the pizza, £20 (about U.S. $32).

Though you may be tempted to try this torturous treat, keep in mind that you have to be at least 18 years old to take part in the challenge. Broderick says you're not missing much: "I've tried it, but I won't be trying it again!"

SCOVILLE HEAT SCALE

- DEATH BY PIZZA CHILIES
- PEPPER SPRAY
- JALAPEÑOS
- TABASCO SAUCE
- BELL PEPPERS

AN OHIO, U.S.A., MAN **SET A RECORD** WHEN HE MADE **206** MEDIUM-SIZE **CHEESE PIZZAS** IN **ONE HOUR.**

A CANADIAN RESTAURANT SELLS AN **$850** (U.S. $680) **PIZZA** TOPPED WITH **LOBSTER,** SMOKED SALMON, **PRAWNS,** AND CAVIAR.

GRAB 'N' GO FOOD

WEIRD FOOD ON WACKY WHEELS

U.S.A.

Street food has long been popular in some countries—have you ever snacked on fried tarantulas in Cambodia? But street eats have only recently gained popularity in the United States, thanks to wacky and delicious food trucks. The Tamale Spaceship's colorfully masked employees—inspired by Mexico's *lucha libre* wrestlers—dish out tamales and guacamole from a silver truck in Chicago, Illinois. In Portland, Oregon, PBJ's Grilled serves peanut butter and jelly sandwiches paired with odd ingredients such as goat cheese, jalapeños, and pickles. And Diggity Doughnuts in Charleston, South Carolina, offers perhaps the craziest flavors ever: salt and pepper, peanut butter and Sriracha hot sauce, and even roasted garlic!

AN EARLY VERSION OF THE **FOOD TRUCK** WAS THE **CHUCK WAGON.** IT *SERVED FOOD* TO **COWBOYS** *MOVING* **CATTLE** ACROSS **PRAIRIES.**

NEWS FEED

>>> CHICAGO, ILLINOIS, AND SAN DIEGO, CALIFORNIA, U.S.A.: STREET FOOD HAS GONE TO THE DOGS—REALLY! THE FOOD TRUCK FIDO TO GO SPECIALIZES IN

84

BOATS BRING ICE CREAM

ENGLAND

What's better than hearing an ice-cream truck jingle on a hot summer day? Seeing this totally awesome ice-cream van float by while you're boating, swimming, or surfing. English ice-cream makers Fredericks created the world's first amphibious ice-cream van to celebrate National Ice Cream Week in England in 2011. It's not the only option for people craving a cold sweet while waterside. A fleet called Ice Cream Boats in the U.K. is expanding to the Mediterranean.

THE **GOOD HUMOR BAR**— **CHOCOLATE-COVERED ICE CREAM** ON A **STICK**— *WAS INVENTED* BY A **CANDYMAKER** WHO FIRST PUT THE **FROZEN TREAT** ON **LOLLIPOP STICKS.**

IN **RURAL ENGLISH VILLAGES** WITHOUT GROCERY STORES, LARGE **VENDING MACHINES** CARRY EVERYTHING FROM **TOILET PAPER** TO **TEA BAGS!**

VERY ODD VENDING MACHINES

VARIOUS LOCATIONS

When Burritoboxes were installed around Los Angeles in 2014, the bright orange vending machines that sell warm, ready-to-eat burritos 24 hours a day (and offer free Wi-Fi while you wait), made U.S. news. Other countries, however, already have a lot more—and a lot weirder—vending machines. Some in China sell live crabs. In Singapore, you can get mashed potatoes and gravy dispensed like a Slurpee. And in Japan, home to the most vending machines per person in the world, you can choose from vegetables, eggs, coffee and tea, rice, hot dogs—you name it!

HEALTHY GOODIES FOR YOUR FOUR-LEGGED FRIENDS. PUPS (AND KITTIES, TOO) CAN CHOOSE FROM MEATY FROZEN YOGURTS, DRIED MEATS, AND BAKED TREATS.

I SCREAM, YOU SCREAM ...

1. GARLIC

2. BROCCOLI AND CHEDDAR

4. PIGS' FEET

5. PEAR AND BLUE CHEESE

3. HONEY CURRY

6. EEL

7. WORMS

8. PIZZA

9. SALT AND PEPPER

10. LIVER AND ONIONS

REAL FLAVOR OR JUST REALLY GROSS?

Do you prefer a lick with a little more ick? Some of these ten wacky flavors are real ice-cream creations you can taste somewhere in the world. Some are just made up. **Can you find the fakes?**

MAKE YOUR OWN
ICE CREAM
IN FIVE MINUTES!

YOU NEED ONLY A COUPLE OF PLASTIC BAGS, A FEW SIMPLE INGREDIENTS, AND A LOT OF SHAKING TO MAKE YOUR OWN TASTY ICE CREAM AT HOME IN MINUTES.

A MAN IN ITALY ONCE **BALANCED** **71 SCOOPS** OF ICE CREAM ON **A CONE!**

SUPPLIES:

1 CUP HALF-AND-HALF
2 TABLESPOONS SUGAR
1/2 TEASPOON VANILLA EXTRACT
1/2 CUP SALT, FOR FREEZING (KOSHER OR ROCK SALT IS BEST, BUT TABLE SALT WILL DO IN A PINCH)
1 PINT-SIZE/SANDWICH-SIZE ZIPLOCK BAG
1 GALLON-SIZE ZIPLOCK BAG
ENOUGH ICE CUBES TO FILL HALF OF THE GALLON-SIZE BAG

DIRECTIONS:

COMBINE THE HALF-AND-HALF, SUGAR, AND VANILLA IN THE SMALLER BAG DON'T FORGET TO SEAL IT! MIX THE ICE AND SALT IN THE LARGER BAG, AND THEN PUT THE SMALLER BAG IN THE LARGER ONE, MAKING SURE THE ICE SURROUNDS THE SMALLER BAG. NOW, SHAKE THE BAGS! IT GETS COLD FAST! SO WEAR GLOVES OR WRAP A TOWEL AROUND THE LARGER BAG TO PROTECT YOUR HANDS. CONTINUE SHAKING FOR ABOUT FIVE MINUTES FOR SOFT ICE CREAM, LONGER FOR HARDER ICE CREAM. VOILÁ! YOU CAN EVEN EAT IT RIGHT OUT OF THE BAG.

ICE-CREAM LICKS = GUITAR LICKS

NEW YORK, NEW YORK, U.S.A.

Live music just got tasty with the invention of an electric ice-cream cone that plays musical tones as you lick the ice cream. The performance is called Lickestra, and two women started it while artists at New York's Visible Futures Lab. In each show, volunteers from the audience step onstage to sit in a white box and play their instrument: a cone that's rigged to make a certain sound—a keyboard or drum track, for example—when the performer's tongue touches the ice cream. At last, a musical instrument you'd love to practice every day!

ENCORE!

ANSWERS: 1. REAL, AVAILABLE AT THE GILROY GARLIC FESTIVAL IN GILROY, CALIFORNIA, U.S.A. 2. FAKE. 3. REAL, AVAILABLE AT ICI IN BERKELEY, CALIFORNIA, U.S.A. 4. REAL, AVAILABLE AT SNOW KING IN TAIPEI, TAIWAN. 5. REAL, AVAILABLE AT SALT & STRAW IN PORTLAND, OREGON, U.S.A. 6. REAL, AVAILABLE AT ICE CREAM CITY IN TOKYO, JAPAN. 7. FAKE. 8. REAL, AVAILABLE AT MAX & MINA'S IN FLUSHING, NEW YORK, U.S.A. 9. REAL, AVAILABLE AT HUMPHRY SLOCOMBE IN SAN FRANCISCO, CALIFORNIA, U.S.A. 10. FAKE.

CHAPTER 5

STRANGE SCIENCE

S FOLLOW DIRECTIONS? • HUMANS COULD RUN
IOUS MONKEY BUSINESS • HOW TO SHRINK T
KROACH NEIGHBORHOODS • THIS VOLCANO'S C
TS A SNOTCOPTER • STRANGE STRUCTURE SOLV
REX POOP? • ANTAR

HATS CONFUSE DUNG BEETLES, PAGE 91

CELESTIAL SCIENCE

DOGS FOLLOW DIRECTIONS?

CZECH REPUBLIC AND GERMANY

You may not watch closely when a dog does its business, but German and Czech scientists did. Working with 70 dogs of 37 different breeds, the scientists recorded 1,893 instances of canines doing their duty, noting which direction they faced while doing so. Surprisingly, they found that under certain conditions, the dogs aligned their bodies north to south—in line with Earth's magnetic field. The dogs still turned their heads, however, to keep a watchful eye on their surroundings while they finished the job.

IN THE UNITED STATES ALONE, **DOGS AND CATS** PRODUCE ABOUT 10 MILLION TONS (9 million MT) OF WASTE A YEAR.

NEWS FEED

>>> **THE MILKY WAY:** GERMAN SCIENTISTS HAVE DISCOVERED THAT OUR GALAXY DOESN SIMPLY FLOAT IN SPACE. INSTEAD, THE STARS WITHIN THE MILKY WAY GENTLY BOB U

HUMANS COULD RUN ON WATER

ROME, ITALY

Scientists in Italy have found a way for people to run across water. They need broad feet and powerful legs. And they need to relocate to someplace with less gravity—like the moon. Studying lizards and aquatic birds, the scientists found that the animals' broad feet spread their weight over a larger area. And their powerful legs push down so hard against the water that it actually pushes back, keeping them afloat. Because of Earth's strong gravitational pull, we can't generate that kind of power. But on the moon, we'd be off to the races.

A *70-POUND* (32-kg) *KID* WOULD WEIGH **12 POUNDS** (5.4 kg) ON THE MOON.

ADULT *DUNG BEETLES* DRINK *THE LIQUID IN THE DUNG THEY FIND; YOUNG DUNG BEETLES* EAT *THE SOLIDS IN IT.*

HATS CONFUSE DUNG BEETLES

SOUTH AFRICA

When dung beetles called "rollers" find a pile of elephant poo, they roll balls of it away to bury and use as a food source for their brood. Rollers travel in a straight line away from the pile to quickly put as much distance as possible between it and themselves. This reduces the chance that other, nearby beetles might steal the ball. Curious how the beetles travel in such straight lines, Swedish biologists took away the insects' main visual cue, the sun, by taping little cardboard hats to rollers' heads. The result? Confused beetles: They wandered aimlessly in circles, never moved away from the doo, and traveled 4.5 times farther than usual.

AND DOWN, MAKING THE GALAXY AS A WHOLE FLUTTER LIKE A FLAG. SCIENTISTS DON'T YET KNOW WHAT CAUSES THE MILKY WAVE.

DIZZY
ICE DISK!

SHEYENNE RIVER, NORTH DAKOTA, U.S.A.

ROUND AND ROUND AND ROUND IT GOES! This circle of ice in the Sheyenne River spun like a record following a cold snap in North Dakota. Arctic air descended on the relatively warm water, say scientists, causing bits of the surface to freeze. The chunks of ice then caught in an eddy (a whirlpool-like current) and began to spin. That movement created a disk of ice that picked up more chunks as it spun, causing the structure to develop growth rings. The disk reached an estimated 55 feet (17 m) across before the river froze it into place.

WHIP SPIDERS SCIENTISTS TRACKING THESE ARACHNIDS LEARNED THEY USE TWO FRONT ANTENNAE-LIKE LEGS TO NAVIGATE DARK COSTA RICAN JUNGLES.

[KEEPING TABS ON ODD ANIMALS]

Scientists stuck tracking devices on these curious critters to learn more about their wild lives.

COLUGOS BACKPACK-LIKE DEVICES SHOWED THESE MAMMALS IN SINGAPORE SAVE ENERGY WHEN THEY WALK RATHER THAN GLIDE THROUGH THE CANOPY.

COLUGOS,
ALSO CALLED
FLYING LEMURS,
USE ENLARGED
SKIN FLAPS
TO GLIDE
BETWEEN
TREETOPS.

LOWLAND TAPIRS RADIO COLLARS HELP RESEARCHERS TRACK SOUTH AMERICA'S HEAVIEST LAND ANIMALS. WHEREVER THESE ANIMALS GO, THEY MAKE A BIG IMPACT—WITH THEIR POOP! THE SEEDS IN IT FROM THE FRUIT THEY'VE EATEN PROMOTE PLANT GROWTH.

RAINBOW FROGS SCIENTISTS DISCOVERED THAT THESE FROGS, FOUND ONLY IN MADAGASCAR, ARE MORE LIKELY TO CLIMB OR BURROW THAN HOP TO A NEW SPOT.

PANGOLIN SCALES
ARE MADE OF
THE SAME STUFF
AS YOUR
FINGERNAILS.

PANGOLINS SCIENTISTS FOUND THAT THESE NOCTURNAL DESERT DWELLERS LIKE TO BORROW ABANDONED AARDVARK BURROWS.

SERIOUS
MONKEY BUSINESS

CHICAGO, ILLINOIS, U.S.A.

Scientists at the University of Chicago have figured out how to stimulate certain cells in monkey brains to make the animals feel as though their fingers had been touched—even though they hadn't. The study may sound silly, but scientists say it's the first step toward developing artificial body parts that would allow wearers to regain a sense of touch.

COCKROACH NEIGHBORHOODS

WHO HIGH SCHOOL STUDENTS, SCIENTISTS

WHAT COLLECTED AND ANALYZED COCKROACH DNA

WHERE NEW YORK, NEW YORK, U.S.A.

HOW NEW YORKERS CAPTURED COCKROACHES AND MAILED THEM TO THE NATIONAL COCKROACH PROJECT. HIGH SCHOOL SLEUTHS THEN HELPED SCIENTISTS STUDY THE ROACHES' DNA.

OUTCOME THE PROJECT REVEALED THAT ROACHES TEND TO STICK TO THEIR OWN PART OF TOWN RATHER THAN MINGLE WITH OTHER ROACHES ELSEWHERE. THIS CREATES COCK-ROACH "NEIGHBORHOODS" THAT AREN'T SO DIFFERENT FROM THE BOROUGHS NEW YORKERS CALL HOME.

NEWS FEED

SCOTLAND: THINK YOU NEED SPECIAL GLASSES TO SEE A MOVIE IN 3-D? STUDY PARTICIPANTS REPORTED THAT CLOSING ONE EYE AND USING

HOW TO SHRINK THE EIFFEL TOWER

ROTTERDAM, THE NETHERLANDS

Leaning to one side can influence your ability to estimate size. Psychologist Anita Eerland had volunteers stand on a Wii Balance Board, then asked them a series of questions while manipulating whether they stood upright or leaned to one side. When people leaned left, they estimated that objects were smaller. The finding is likely due to our tendency to read numbers in sequential order from left to right (such as 0, 1, 2, etc.).

LEAN LEFT, LOOKS SMALLER

YAWNING IS DOGGONE CONTAGIOUS

TOKYO, JAPAN

Ever catch yourself yawning just because someone else did? Scientists think such contagious yawns are a sign of emotional attachment—even between a dog and its owner! Japanese researchers recorded whether dogs yawned in response to seeing their owner yawn or a stranger yawn. The dogs were more likely to do so with their owner than a stranger.

THE OTHER TO PEER AT A PHOTO THROUGH A PEA-SIZE HOLE MADE THE IMAGE APPEAR THREE-DIMENSIONAL.

THIS
VOLCANO'S GOT

YELLOW SULFUR CREATES BLUE HUE

THERE ARE ABOUT **1,500 VOLCANOES ON EARTH** THAT COULD *ERUPT.*

LAVA'S **COLOR** DEPENDS ON ITS **TEMPERATURE.** BRIGHT ORANGE LAVA IS THE HOTTEST—IT CAN REACH 2,280 DEGREES FAHRENHEIT (1,250 degrees Celsius).

THE BLUES

INDONESIA

Welcome to Kawah Ijen volcano in Indonesia, w glows an eerie blue at night. This bizarre spe occurs thanks to high levels of sulfur inside t mountain. Superheated sulfuric gases escape volcano through cracks in its surface. When those gase come into contact with air, they burst into blue flames. glowing streams flowing down the side of the volcano ar lava—they're rivers of liquid sulfur. The fluid formed fro flaming gases then falls to the surface like rain.

The sulfur content on Kawah Ijen is high enough that miners risk their health when they collect large chunks o mineral. Two to three times a day, the miners hike into th crater of the volcano, exposing themselves to harmful ga They cart out heavy loads of sulfur—as much as 220 poun (100 kg) per visit. The sulfur is used to make matches and fertilizer, refine sugar, and vulcanize rubber, a process tha involves adding sulfur to sticky natural rubber in order to make it stronger and better able to handle heat and cold.

As weird as it may be, Kawah Ijen isn't the only volcano glows blue. Dallol volcano in Ethiopia also does, as did Italy' Mount Vesuvius in ancient times.

THOSE HUGE (AND HEAVY!) CHUNKS OF SULFUR DON'T EARN MINERS MUCH—LESS THAN 25 CENTS PER POUND (AROUND $5 A DAY).

EAR MITES ARE ABOUT THE SIZE OF A **HEAD OF A PIN.**

ITCHY EXPERIMENT

Wanting to know whether cat ear mites could also infest humans, a veterinarian put them in his own ear and recorded his experience. The infestation cleared up on its own after several weeks, causing the veterinarian to wonder whether his results might have been "flawed or misleading." So to be sure, he repeated the experiment—twice! Each case cleared up faster than the one before as his body built up immunity, or protection, against the itchy critters.

1994

INVISIBLE GORILLA

When people pay attention to one thing, they sometimes miss other things happening around them. To see just how "blind" we can be, scientists asked volunteers to count the number of basketball passes among two teams of people. One team wore white, the other black. Volunteers watching the team dressed in white failed to notice when a man in a black gorilla suit walked through—even though he stopped mid-game to thump his chest!

2004

>>> THE IG NOBEL PRIZES: HONORING STRANGE

The Ig Nobel Prizes are awarded annually to honor strange science. The "Ig" stands for ignoble, which means "not honorable."

2000

Scientists in the Netherlands discovered that nonmagnetic objects placed in a strong magnetic field would levitate, or float. They tested their discovery on all types of items—even frogs! When the magnetic force is strong enough, it repels an object's atoms, causing it to defy gravity.

FLOATING FROGS

BUBBLE
BABBLE

2004

Herring, a type of fish, can hear. To find out what the fish are listening for, biologists in Canada and Scotland watched the animals closely. They discovered that herring use sound to communicate with each other. But the fish don't use their mouths to chat. Instead, they release bursts of bubbles from their bums! The scientists call the bursts "fast repetitive ticks," or FRTs. Who says science isn't a gas?

SNOTCOPTER

2010

Just like people, whales get sick. Scientists wanted to be able to check the massive marine mammals' health, but taking their temperature is no easy task. So scientists attached petri dishes to the landing gear of a remote-controlled helicopter and then flew it through a whale's exhaled spray. The snot-covered dishes gave the scientists just the germs they were looking for to find out if the whales were well.

STRANGE STRUCTURE *SOLVED?*

MYSTERY IN THE AMAZON

TAMBOPATA, PERU

Like an Amazon version of crop circles, these bizarre fenced-in towers appear only on a small island in the Peruvian rain forest. When they were first discovered, no one had a clue what might have created them. The tiny, mysterious structures (less than 1 inch—about 2 cm—across) became an Internet sensation as experts weighed in on what might have built them. Guesses ranged from spiders to insects such as lacewings and moths.

But guesses don't get answers. So a team of entomologists, or insect scientists, returned to the jungle to solve the mystery. It took days and nights of patient observation, but they finally cracked the case: A single spiderling, or baby spider, hatched from each of three towers.

Many spiders keep watch over their egg sacs, which eventually release large numbers of spiderlings. So finding the baby spiders on their own surprised the observers. Because this spider species isn't familiar to scientists, they don't yet know the purpose of the fence. It may trap mites for the spiderling's first meal or keep predatory ants out. The mystery still isn't totally solved, but scientists are sticking with it.

A **SINGLE** SPIDER EGG SAC CAN CONTAIN AS MANY AS **600** EGGS.

A TINY MITE GETS TANGLED UP—FOR A FUTURE MEAL?

A SUPERSMALL SPIDERLING GOES IT ALONE AFTER HATCHING FROM ITS EGG IN THE STRUCTURE.

SPIDER EGG **SACS** LAID OUTSIDE COME IN GREEN, BROWN, AND RED HUES TO BLEND IN.

MAN GROWS NOSE
ON FOREHEAD

FUJIAN PROVINCE, CHINA

When this man's nose was damaged by injury and infection, doctors decided to grow him a new one. Using cartilage from his rib cage and expanding the skin on the man's forehead, they constructed the new nose where it would be easiest to move into place.

CENTURIES-OLD MUMMY!

ANTARCTIC SEAL MUMMIES

WHAT 300 MUMMIFIED SEALS

WHERE MCMURDO DRY VALLEYS, ANTARCTICA

HOW THE DRY VALLEYS ARE SO DRY—GETTING LESS THAN HALF AN INCH (1.3 CM) OF PRECIPITATION A YEAR—THAT SEALS THAT WANDER INTO THE DESERT FREEZE-DRY INSTEAD OF DECOMPOSE.

WHY SCIENTISTS AREN'T SURE WHY THE SEALS WIND UP IN THE VALLEYS. THEY MAY HAVE SIMPLY TAKEN A WRONG TURN.

OUTCOME STUDYING THE SEALS, WHICH RANGE FROM 500 TO 5,000 YEARS OLD, ALLOWS SCIENTISTS TO LEARN MORE ABOUT HOW THE ANTARCTIC CLIMATE HAS CHANGED.

NEWS FEED

>>> **ALBERTA, CANADA:** TO RESTORE ORDER TO UNHEALTHY GUTS, SCIENTISTS HAVE TAKEN BACTERIA FROM HEALTHY PEOPLE'S POOP AND PACKED IT INTO

CHIMPS, *CHAMPIONS OF* REAR RECOGNITION

ATLANTA, GEORGIA, U.S.A.

Chimpanzees have distinctive rear ends—so much so that scientists decided to see whether the apes use them to identify each other. When researchers showed chimpanzees pictures of their group-mates' faces and bums, the chimps correctly matched the mug to the rump. The discovery gives a whole new meaning to the term two-faced!

YOU LOOK FAMILIAR

T. REX POOP?

SASKATCHEWAN, CANADA

What's 17 inches (44 cm) long, full of bones, and big enough to overflow a two-liter bottle? Dino poop. Bone fragments fill nearly half of this fossilized feces, leading scientists to think it may have come from a *Tyrannosaurus rex*. It's the only meat-eating dino that lived where the feces was found.

A PILL. IT MAY BE UNAPPEALING, BUT IT'S THE LATEST, LEAST GROSS WAY TO FIGHT SEVERE INTESTINAL INFECTION. AND IT WORKS!

WHAT IN THE WORLD IS THIS?

These incredible close-ups were produced by high-powered scanning electron microscopes. Can you guess what these images actually are? Only one of the three answers for each image is right. Choose carefully: To make details easier to see, colors have been added—though they aren't necessarily the same ones actually found on the object. You'll find the answers at the bottom of the page.

1.

A. moth tongue
B. beetle antenna
C. fly foot

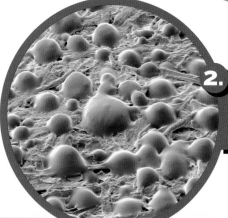

2.

A. pond slime
B. sticky note glue
C. octopus suckers

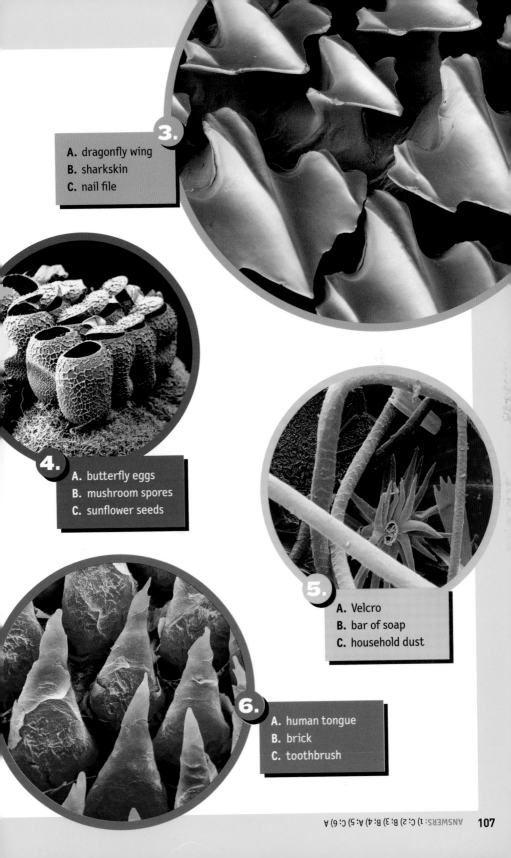

3.
A. dragonfly wing
B. sharkskin
C. nail file

4.
A. butterfly eggs
B. mushroom spores
C. sunflower seeds

5.
A. Velcro
B. bar of soap
C. household dust

6.
A. human tongue
B. brick
C. toothbrush

CHAPTER 6

WAY-OUT TRAVEL

GHOULISH GOLLUM, PAGE 115

A JAR-iNG TOURiST DESTiNATiON!

PHONSAVAN, LAOS

Cereal bowls to the giants? Ancient witches' brew kettles? Mystery still surrounds the origin of the massive stone jars that dot the rolling hills of northeastern Laos. The hundreds of artifacts make up the Plain of Jars, one of Laos's most popular tourist attractions. Archaeologists say these jars are around 2,000 years old. One legend suggests that a king brewed celebratory beverages in them. Whatever their purpose, one thing is certain: The Plain of Jars is just plain weird.

ONE PACKED POOL!

ROOM FOR ONE MORE?

SICHUAN PROVINCE, CHINA

No, those aren't ants invading a bowl of breakfast cereal. Those colorful rings are actually inner tubes occupied by vacationers in what might be the most crowded swimming pool ever. About 15,000 people packed this 323,000-square-foot (30,000-sq-m) park's saltwater pool on this hot summer day in 2013. Can it still be called a swimming pool even if there's no room to swim?

NEW MEANING OF "AIRPLANE FOOD"

WHAT THE 118-SEAT LA TANTE DC 10 RESTAURANT, WHICH LOCALS CALL THE GREEN PLANE

WHY THE OWNERS FOUND A NEW USE FOR AN OLD AIRPLANE THAT STOPPED FLYING IN 2005 WHEN THE AIRLINE RAN OUT OF MONEY.

WHEN OPENED IN 2013

WHERE ACCRA, GHANA

OUTCOME THE GREEN PLANE, WITH A PICTURE OF GHANA'S FLAG PAINTED ON ITS TAIL, IS POPULAR,

BUT NOT JUST FOR THE FOOD. REPORTEDLY, LOCALS ENJOY TOURING THE INSIDE OF THE AIRCRAFT, SINCE MANY OF THEM HAVE NEVER FLOWN.

La Tante DC 10 Restaurant
Welcome aboard Charlie
CLUB

NEWS FEED

>>> **MELBOURNE, AUSTRALIA:** WATCH WHERE YOU'RE WALKING! IN 2013, A TAIWANESE TOURIST WALKED OFF AN AUSTRALIAN PIER WHILE CHECKING

WISH YOU WERE HERE!

TOKYO, JAPAN

Ever wonder how bored your stuffed animals must be while you're in school? Treat them to a vacation with Unagi Travel, a Tokyo-based agency whose only clients are your fuzzy friends! Owner Sonoe Azuma takes them on a tour of Tokyo's sights, to bathe in hot springs, or to a surprise mystery destination. Stuffed animals send their owners a postcard, and the agency even posts trip photos to the Internet.

AWESOME IN-FLIGHT ENTERTAINMENT

SYDNEY, AUSTRALIA

Passengers boarding Virgin Australia Flight 097 from Brisbane to Sydney were treated to a performance that beats safety videos any day: The touring cast of *The Lion King*, who filled the first few rows, spontaneously burst into song! The group enthusiastically belted out "Circle of Life," complete with hand claps. Later that year, the cast of the Broadway production burst into song while riding the subway in New York City!

A PLAY ON A PLANE!

A POPULAR SOCIAL NETWORKING SITE ON HER PHONE. THE WOMAN, WHO COULDN'T SWIM, ENDED UP IN THE HOSPITAL AFTER THE ABSENTMINDED ACCIDENT.

BEIJING CAPITAL INTERNATIONAL AIRPORT, CHINA FIVE "FUWA" ROBOTS—BASED ON THE BEIJING OLYMPIC MASCOTS—ANSWER TRAVELERS' QUESTIONS.

[WHILE YOU WAIT ...]

You've probably never wished for a canceled flight. But crazy, cool features at airports around the world can make the journey as exciting as the destination!

SAN FRANCISCO INTERNATIONAL AIRPORT, CALIFORNIA, U.S.A. DO YOGA TO UNWIND AFTER A LONG FLIGHT.

SCHIPHOL AIRPORT, AMSTERDAM, THE NETHERLANDS FLIERS PASSING THROUGH CAN RENT A LITTLE ROOM FOR A LITTLE SHUT-EYE.

ABOUT
7,000
AIRCRAFT ARE IN U.S. SKIES AT ANY GIVEN TIME.

CHANGI AIRPORT, SINGAPORE SLIP DOWN THE WORLD'S TALLEST AIRPORT SLIDE—FOUR STORIES!—DURING A STOPOVER.

MORE THAN **94 MILLION PEOPLE** PASS THROUGH **ATLANTA, GEORGIA, U.S.A.'S INTERNATIONAL AIRPORT—** THE **WORLD'S BUSIEST** PASSENGER **AIRPORT— EVERY YEAR.**

TWICE THE WACKY WAIT!

CHANGI AIRPORT, SINGAPORE FAKE ICE-SKATING IS REAL FUN!

WELLINGTON AIRPORT, NEW ZEALAND *THE LORD OF THE RINGS'* GHOULISH GOLLUM WATCHES OVER PASSENGERS.

115

CROSS-COUNTRY
TIME TRAVELERS!

ANDALUSIA, SPAIN, AND ALGARVE, PORTUGAL

The world's first cross-country zip line, LimiteZero, opened in late 2013 between Spain and Portugal. Brave riders zip 43 miles an hour (70 km/h) high above the river that divides the two countries. Sound scary? Don't worry: All riders, who must be at least 14 years old, are required to wear a safety harness. Still unsure whether to try it? How about the chance to travel back in time? Because of the time difference between the countries, riders gain an hour when they land in Portugal!

PORTUGAL

SPAIN

BIZARRE FOOD
MUSEUMS

FRENCH
FRY FUN

BRUGES, BELGIUM

Is there a better food than french fries? Father and son Eddy and Cedric Van Belle don't think so. In 2013, they opened the world's first museum dedicated entirely to fried potatoes. Housed in the oldest building in Bruges, the museum contains some 400 artifacts, artwork, and history having to do with french fries, plus the chance to sample them. An educational excuse to eat fries? Pass the ketchup (and mayo), please!

THE LARGEST EVER **SERVING** OF **FRENCH FRIES** WEIGHED MORE THAN A **GRIZZLY BEAR.**

NEWS FEED

GUADALEST, SPAIN: THERE ARE MORE THAN 20,000 SALT AND PEPPER SHAKERS ON DISPLAY IN THE SALT AND PEPPER SHAKER MUSEUM IN

KIWIS GROW ON VINES, LIKE GRAPES.

CUCKOO FOR KIWIS

TE PUKE, NEW ZEALAND

Don't confuse kiwis, those fuzzy brown berries you see at the supermarket, with Kiwis, an international nickname for people from New Zealand. You'll see a lot of both at Kiwi360, a park dedicated to the fruit. And what better way to do so than aboard a KiwiKart? This kooky, kiwi-shaped tram takes visitors on a 40-minute tour of the more than 50 varieties of the fruit grown on the property. At the end, visitors can sample some of the kiwis and have their photo taken inside a four-story steel-and-fiberglass kiwi slice.

ABOUT 800 MILLION SERVINGS OF CURRYWURST ARE SOLD IN GERMANY EACH YEAR.

WHERE CURRYWURST IS THE BEST

BERLIN, GERMANY

You may not have heard of currywurst, a German fast food of sliced sausage traditionally topped with curry ketchup. But in Berlin, the food is so popular that it has its own museum. A sensory experience, the Deutsches Currywurst Museum offers visitors a spice-sniffing station, the chance to listen to songs about currywurst, and a sausage-shaped sofa to relax on. You'll want to make time for a snack at the end: The café offers currywurst (pork, chicken, or veggie) topped with your choice of sauces.

SPAIN. THE TOWN WHERE YOU'LL FIND THEM, HOWEVER, HAS ONLY 200 PEOPLE—THAT'S 1/100 THE NUMBER OF SHAKERS!

BEAR
NECESSITIES

CHINA OPENS FIRST
PANDA-THEMED HOTEL

NEWBORN **PANDAS** ARE **PINK** AND **HAIRLESS.**

PANDAS SPEND AT LEAST **12 HOURS** OF EVERY DAY **EATING** BAMBOO.

LUNCH WITH PANDAS!

SLEEP WITH PANDAS!

DRINK TEA WITH PANDAS!

EMEISHAN, CHINA

Cute doesn't even begin to describe the Panda Inn—it's downright adorable. Beds are covered in panda pillows. Panda paintings adorn the walls. Staff dress in full plush panda costumes. There are only 32 rooms, each with its own theme-within-a-theme such as anime, space, forest, and dance. And the real-deal pandas are only a couple of hours away by car. The hotel sits at the base of Emei Mountain, a popular destination for those who want to catch a glimpse of rare giant pandas at the Chengdu Research Base of Giant Panda Breeding.

SHORT
SUBWAY
RIDE

1870

Inventor Alfred Ely Beach built New York City's first subway: a short, 300-foot (91-m) ride in a tunnel beneath Broadway. High-powered fans at each end helped blast subway cars back and forth. And locals were just as excited to see the tunnel as they were to ride the underground train. You can't take the trip today: The tunnel was destroyed to make way for another.

>>> WACKY WAYS TO GET AROUND

1960s

CHICKEN
BUSES

American school buses are usually retired after 8 to 12 years, or about 150,000 miles (241,402 km). But that isn't always the end of the road for them. Guatemalans sometimes buy the buses, paint brightly colored murals on them, and use them as public transportation. Many of these vehicles, also called "chicken buses" because of how packed they get, have been around for half a century. Though a bumpy, sometimes sweaty ride, they're an affordable, colorful way to see Central America!

THE LONGEST
BUS RIDE
EVER WAS
54,289 MILES
(87,367 KM)
THROUGH
18 COUNTRIES
IN **13** MONTHS!

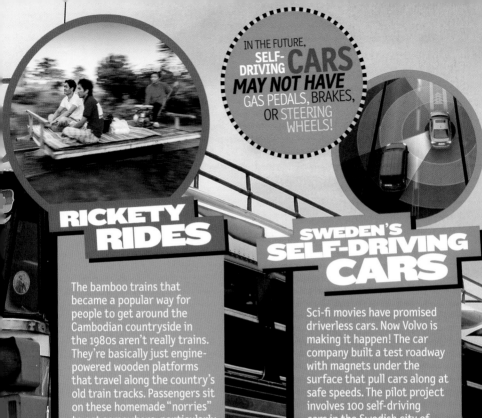

IN THE FUTURE, **SELF-DRIVING CARS** *MAY NOT HAVE* GAS PEDALS, BRAKES, OR STEERING WHEELS!

RICKETY RIDES

1980s

The bamboo trains that became a popular way for people to get around the Cambodian countryside in the 1980s aren't really trains. They're basically just engine-powered wooden platforms that travel along the country's old train tracks. Passengers sit on these homemade "norries" to get somewhere, particularly if they have cargo to carry. In Cambodia's capital, things are becoming more modern: In 2014, Phnom Penh got its first public buses.

SWEDEN'S SELF-DRIVING CARS

2014

Sci-fi movies have promised driverless cars. Now Volvo is making it happen! The car company built a test roadway with magnets under the surface that pull cars along at safe speeds. The pilot project involves 100 self-driving cars in the Swedish city of Goteborg. Bad weather and other unpredictable problems such as traffic are no match for this track's ability to keep things moving!

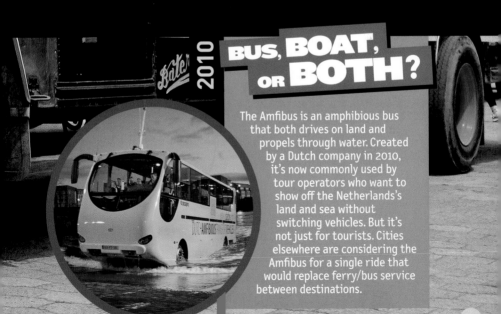

2010

BUS, BOAT, OR BOTH?

The Amfibus is an amphibious bus that both drives on land and propels through water. Created by a Dutch company in 2010, it's now commonly used by tour operators who want to show off the Netherlands's land and sea without switching vehicles. But it's not just for tourists. Cities elsewhere are considering the Amfibus for a single ride that would replace ferry/bus service between destinations.

DANXIA LANDFORMS, CHINA LAYERS OF SANDSTONE AND OTHER MINERALS FORM A ROCKY RAINBOW.

[FOLLOW THE RAINBOW]

Reds and yellows and blues, oh my! These vacation spots may make you do a double take. But they're all real and all really cool.

UKRAINE TRAINS AND SWEETHEARTS PASS THROUGH THIS LEAFY "TUNNEL OF LOVE."

URAL MOUNTAINS, RUSSIA SNOW-TOPPED TREES RESEMBLE SNOWMEN ALONG THE SIBERIAN BORDER.

THE LAYERS OF THE
DANXIA LANDFORMS
WERE CREATED OVER
24 MILLION YEARS
AND BUCKLED BY
TECTONIC PLATES.

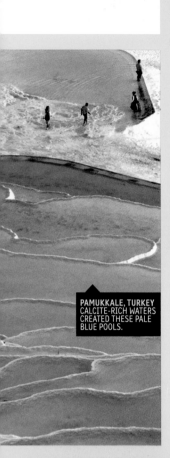

PAMUKKALE, TURKEY CALCITE-RICH WATERS CREATED THESE PALE BLUE POOLS.

LAKE NATRON, TANZANIA ALGAE GIVE THIS SUPERSALTY LAKE ITS CREEPY COLOR.

MORE THAN **2 MILLION**
LESSER **FLAMINGOS**
VISIT **LAKE NATRON**
ANNUALLY.

NAMIB-NAUKLUFT NATIONAL PARK, NAMIBIA MORNING SUNLIGHT TINTS A SKY-HIGH SAND DUNE ORANGE.

THE
FUTURE
OF

It may look like a space shuttle, but this beast is actually a model of what could be the biggest airplane to ever fly the friendly skies. Designer Oscar Viñals's AWWA Sky Whale would use advanced technologies to create a smooth flight that's better for the environment—and for the approximately 755 people on board! The Sky Whale is not ready to take wing just yet: At this point it's only a carefully researched idea and illustration. But keep your fingers crossed for a trip on this fancy ride in the future.

FLYING?

WACKY ROAD TRIP

PHEASANTS ON THE PRAIRIE
Regent, North Dakota, U.S.A.

These big birds, or "Pheasants on the Prairie," are actually giant metal sculptures perched along the Enchanted Highway.

How Weird Is Your Family Vacation?
Road trips generally lead to one question: "Are we there yet?" Kill some time by using this bingo card to keep track of all the crazy things you see from your seat. Use a coin to cover the square when you see one of these silly sights. If you see all six, your vacation truly is weird but true!

LIFE ON MARS
Pennsylvania, U.S.A.

To find out what life is like on Mars, you don't have to leave Earth. Just drive through this small town with a silly name.

SILLY CITY NAME	WEIRD ROADSIDE ATTRACTION	FUNNY LICENSE PLATE
ODD ANIMAL SIGHTING	CRAZY ROADSIDE RESTAURANT	UNUSUAL VEHICLE

TOPSY-TURVY HOUSE
Terfens, Austria

You're not imagining things—that really is a house built upside down! A pair of Polish architects built this topsy-turvy tourist attraction in 2012.

TURTLE CAFÉ
Gobi, Mongolia

Have you ever wanted to eat inside of a two-story turtle? Diners can do just that at this Bayanzag ("flaming cliffs") tourist camp restaurant.

GOATS IN TREES
Morocco

That's no partridge in a pear tree—it's a goat in an argan tree! The animals go to great heights to find food in the desert. Odd animal sighting, indeed!

TAIL-WAGGING WELCOME
Tirau, New Zealand

A wacky-shaped information center welcomes visitors to this artsy town. They can also check out the big sheep-shaped wool shop next door.

CHAPTER 7

WEIRD
WORLD OF
SPORTS

BALL FANS CREATE EARTH-SHAKING NOISE • SWI
TAROD • BOBSLEDDER BUSTS OUT • CLIMBING T
RNATIONAL CAMEL AND OSTRICH RACES • BRIN
NFR • TRACK STAR NAILS IT • GOOFY GRIN • CL
PICTURE PERFECT • YOU PLA

OSTRICH RACES, PAGE 139

FOOTBALL FANS CREATE EARTH-SHAKING NOISE

SEATTLE, WASHINGTON, U.S.A.

Seattle Seahawks fans are so noisy that in 2011, 2013, and 2014, their cheering and stomping during games against the New Orleans Saints registered as small earthquakes! During the 2013 game, Seahawks fans' stadium-size enthusiasm measured as a magnitude 1 or 2 quake. And they were nearly as loud as a jet engine 100 feet (30 m) away!

BOBSLEDDER BUSTS OUT

WHO AMERICAN BOBSLEDDER JOHNNY QUINN

WHERE SOCHI 2014 WINTER OLYMPICS

WHAT BUSTED THROUGH A BATHROOM DOOR, LEAVING A HUGE HOLE BEHIND, WHEN HE GOT STUCK INSIDE AND HIS TEAM MEMBERS COULDN'T HEAR HIM BANGING TO GET OUT.

HOW QUINN SAYS HE USED HIS BOBSLED PUSH TRAINING TO PUNCH A BIG ENOUGH HOLE IN THE DOOR TO SQUEEZE HIS 6-FOOT (1.8-M), 220-POUND (100-KG) FRAME THROUGH.

OUTCOME NEWS OF THE BREAKOUT SPREAD AFTER THE OLYMPIAN POSTED THIS PHOTO TO HIS TWITTER ACCOUNT. AND

WHILE IT'S WEIRD TO GET STUCK IN A BATHROOM, WHAT HAPPENED A FEW DAYS LATER IS EVEN WEIRDER: QUINN GOT STUCK AGAIN, THIS TIME IN AN ELEVATOR WITH HIS TEAMMATE NICK CUNNINGHAM!

NEWS FEED

MOUNT EVEREST, NEPAL: THE WORLD'S HIGHEST MOUNTAIN IS GETTING A MAKEOVER: A NEW LAW REQUIRES CLIMBERS TO PICK UP MORE THAN

SWIMMER *PULLS* TON OF BRICKS, *LITERALLY*

FANCY FLIPPER!

DETROIT, MICHIGAN, U.S.A.

In 2013, Jim Dreyer attempted to swim 22 miles (35 km) in Lake St. Clair while pulling two little boats loaded with 334 bricks that together weighed a ton (907 kg). One boat sank about a third of the way into the trip. And Dreyer reportedly started hallucinating from exhaustion and even got lost. But he did it all for a good cause: Each brick was signed by the swimmer and then sold to benefit the homebuilding charity Habitat for Humanity.

IDITAROD *VERSUS* IDIOTAROD

NEW YORK, NEW YORK, U.S.A.

You've probably heard of the Iditarod, the famous Alaskan dogsled race. But what about the Idiotarod—the contest where people wear crazy costumes and push shopping carts through city streets? Organizers of the dogsled race weren't thrilled with the name similarity. So they sent a cease and desist order to Idiotarod coordinators, forcing them to change the event's name. In 2014, the Idiotarod officially became the Idiotarodorama. Try saying that five times fast!

17 POUNDS (8 KG) OF GARBAGE ALONG THEIR ROUTE. THAT WASTE WEIGHT IS IN ADDITION TO THE GEAR AND FOOD CLIMBERS CARRY.

CLIMBING THE WALLS!

LOOK MA, NO ROPES!

ALEX HONNOLD **LIVES** IN A **VAN** **EQUIPPED WITH** A **STOVE, BED, STORAGE** FOR CLIMBING GEAR, AND A **SOLAR PANEL** FOR CHARGING **ELECTRONICS.**

POTRERO CHICO, MEXICO

Some say he's crazy. But Alex Honnold just chooses to live life on the edge—by climbing to dizzying heights without wearing any protective harnesses or ropes!

Honnold got his start rock climbing in a gym around age ten. He didn't make his first climb without safety equipment, called free soloing, until the age of 19 or 20. Now, he travels the world doing what he loves most: scaling really steep mountains. Though he's perhaps best known for his free solo climbs in California, U.S.A.'s Yosemite National Park, he recently scrambled up the 2,500-foot (762-m) face of El Sendero Luminoso in Mexico in just over three hours. The video filmed during that climb is crazy: Honnold looks like little more than a fly on a wall!

Over time, he's learned how to manage fears that come up while climbing. Still, you might be surprised to hear, he's afraid of snakes—but only the dangerous kinds. "Things like snakes and bugs have always made me a bit uncomfortable, but I wouldn't say they scare me. Unless it's a cobra or a python, then it is actually scary because a real danger exists."

HONNOLD **CLIMBED** YOSEMITE NATIONAL PARK'S **HALF DOME— 2,130 FEET** (649 M) OF **VERTICAL GRANITE**— *WITHOUT* ANY **SAFETY DEVICES.**

DANGLING FROM AN OVERHANG IN THE MUSANDAM PENINSULA IN OMAN

SCALING THE MOONLIGHT BUTTRESS IN UTAH'S ZION NATIONAL PARK

RING OF

FLAMING TETHERBALL IS FAST, HOT, AND DANGEROUS

SEATTLE, WASHINGTON, U.S.A.

It's all in the name: flaming tetherball. This crazy (and admittedly unsafe) game was invented by a group of artists who call themselves Hazard Factory, fittingly. Instead of a traditional tetherball, players use a fireball. And instead of their hands, they hit the flaming orb with tennis rackets, scoring a point each time they make contact. Don't try this at home! Players must wear safety gear to protect themselves. And even then, this is a sport best left to the "professionals."

A GAME OF FLAMING TETHERBALL ENDS WHEN THE FIREBALL DIES OUT, WHICH USUALLY TAKES ABOUT 5 MINUTES.

FIRE

A STORMTROOPER
HELMET DOUBLES AS
PROTECTIVE GEAR!

WACKY
WORLD
RACES

ANTARCTIC ICE MARATHON

ANTARCTICA

There's not much you can do to completely prepare for this southernmost race on Earth, which covers a 26.2-mile (42.2-km) frozen route. Still, some participants try— by training inside of a meat locker! The race is held in November, during the Antarctic summer, but runners still battle blinding snow glare, frozen sweat, and the threat of frostbite. Competitors who make it through the marathon and have competed in races on the six other continents win a desirable spot in the Seven Continents Club.

ANTARCTICA IS A **DESERT:** THE LITTLE SNOW IT GETS **DOESN'T MELT,** BUT RATHER JUST **BUILDS UP** INTO ICE SHEETS.

NEWS FEED

>>> LONDON, ENGLAND: AT THE 2014 LONDON MARATHON, RUNNERS SET MORE THAN TWO DOZEN WACKY WORLD RECORDS, INCLUDING THE

INTERNATIONAL CAMEL & OSTRICH RACES

ALTHOUGH OSTRICHES CAN'T FLY, THEY CAN SPRINT UP TO 43 MILES (70 km/h) AN HOUR!

VIRGINIA CITY, NEVADA, U.S.A.

As far as wacky races go, this one may take the cake! Every year, thousands of people head to Virginia City's International Camel & Ostrich Races, in which human jockeys ride camels, ostriches, and zebras. Even the event's history is odd: After a newspaper journalist wrote a fake story in 1959 about camel races, the city decided to actually hold one. Those 18 or older can get in on the fun: Simply pay $500 for a sponsorship package that includes a safety class and a chance to be the jockey!

SAN FRANCISCO'S **VERMONT STREET** IS **STEEPER** THOUGH **LESS CURVY** THAN THE CITY'S FAMOUSLY CROOKED **LOMBARD STREET.**

BRING YOUR OWN BIG WHEEL

SAN FRANCISCO, CALIFORNIA, U.S.A.

Think of this race as a real-life version of Mario Kart. At the Bring Your Own Big Wheel (or BYOBW) race, held each Easter Sunday, costumed people ride Big Wheel trikes down San Francisco's steep and curvy Vermont and 20th Streets. Though there's one heat for kids 12 and under, the others are for all ages and mostly feature grown-ups who are much too big to steer the toys. Space is very limited, but it's free to participate. Just BYOBW (and helmet and safety pads).

FASTEST FINISHES DRESSED AS A TOILET, ANIMAL, ASTRONAUT, COWBOY, BRIDE, MONK, TV CHARACTER, BABY, DOCTOR, NURSE, FIREFIGHTER, AND PLAYING CARD.

EVERY TWO YEARS, **WOMEN** IN TRADITIONAL GREEK DRESS **USE ONLY** THE SUN AND A MIRROR **TO LIGHT** THE **OLYMPIC FLAME** IN OLYMPIA.

NAKED OLYMPIANS!

776 B.C.

The Olympics have changed a lot since their debut in ancient Greece. Perhaps the biggest difference between now and then: The first Olympic athletes competed in their birthday suits! Today's uniforms may be ultratight, but at least they offer some protection and privacy.

TRACK STAR NAILS IT

1996

Gail Devers's medal wasn't the only gold she wore during the 1996 Summer Games in Atlanta, Georgia, U.S.A. The U.S. track star also sported extraordinarily long gold fingernails. Devers was already known for her attention-grabbing accessories, having rocked long and colorful nails at the 1992 games, too.

>>> ODD OLYMPIC FASHION

1960

BAREFOOT WINNER

Ethiopian Abebe Bikila ran a record-breaking Olympic marathon—without wearing any shoes! His team-issued pair for the Rome, Italy, games was causing blisters, so he took to the course sans shoes, which was often how he trained anyway. His race time—2 hours, 15 minutes, and 16 seconds—not only was the fastest ever, but it also earned Bikila the honor of being the first black African to win a gold medal.

CURLERS' CRAZY CLOTHES

2014

Who knew the sport of curling could look even odder? In 2014, Norway's curling team showed up in Sochi, Russia, wearing some of the craziest outfits ever. The athletes wore a different pair of patterned pants—such as plaid, striped, rose-printed, or houndstooth— for each of nine games. They had to repeat a pair of pants for their tenth game, which they lost to Great Britain. Lesson learned for next time?

2012

GOLD MEDALIST'S GOOFY GRIN

Some athletes show their style with unique outfits. But U.S. swimmer Ryan Lochte showed off a custom-made mouthpiece decorated in diamonds and rubies after he won his gold medal at the 2012 Olympics in London. (Game officials reportedly forbade him from wearing it on the podium.) The guy who made the grill, which looked like the American flag, says it cost around $25,000, though he notes he gave Lochte the "Olympic discount."

PiCTURE PERFECT

WEIRD-SPORTS PHOTOGRAPHER HAS BEST JOB EVER!

PORTLAND, OREGON, U.S.A.

Sol Neelman is one cool dude. His love of sports, traveling, and fun has led him to a career of trekking around the world to photograph sports—weird sports, specifically.

Neelman realized in 2005 that he loved strange sports more than other sporting events, even the Olympics. That year he started shooting pictures of everything from Roller Derby to underwater hockey to dog surfing. Eventually, he had enough images to put together a book called *Weird Sports.* Its sequel, *Weird Sports 2,* was published in 2014.

Neelman says his favorite sport is Kaiju Big Battel, a form of entertainment wrestling between people dressed in monster costumes that is popular in Japan. He's still waiting for a chance to photograph SlamBall ("basketball with trampolines," he explains) and Ultimate Tazer Ball, which is as scary as it sounds. Says Neelman, it's a "form of rugby with low-level Tasers. Yes, Tasers!" (The Tasers have since been downgraded to stun guns).

Neelman never imagined that what started as a side project would turn into his actual job. "If I had any advice for kids, it'd be to always follow your passions—whatever those are—and never, ever slow down."

And even if you aren't athletic, you can still stay involved in sports, he says. "I was never very good at sports, but I've always loved following them."

THE **WOZ** CHALLENGE CUP, OR **SEGWAY POLO** WORLD CHAMPIONSHIP, IS NAMED FOR **FAN**, **PLAYER**, AND **APPLE** CO-FOUNDER **STEVE WOZNIAK**.

SOL NEELMAN SHOOTS THE COLOR RUN IN SEATTLE.

HOO-AH! AMERICAN KURTIS ROBERTS GIVES IT HIS BEST SHOT (PUT) AT THE U.S. OLYMPIC TRACK AND FIELD TRIALS.

[ATHLETES CAUGHT ON CAMERA!]

Professional athletes focus more on winning than looking good for the camera, as these funny in-the-moment photos show!

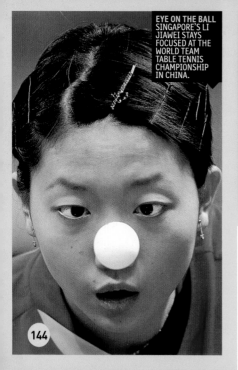

EYE ON THE BALL SINGAPORE'S LI JIAWEI STAYS FOCUSED AT THE WORLD TEAM TABLE TENNIS CHAMPIONSHIP IN CHINA.

GAME FACE MARCOS BAGHDATIS OF CYPRUS KEEPS HIS EYES ON THE PRIZE DURING THE SYDNEY INTERNATIONAL TENNIS TOURNAMENT IN AUSTRALIA.

DURING AN OLYMPIC TABLE TENNIS MATCH, **BALLS** *CAN REACH SPEEDS* OF UP TO **100 MILES** (160 KM/H) AN HOUR.

PHOTO FINISH JAMAICA'S SHELLY-ANN FRASER-PRYCE MAKES A FACE WHILE WINNING THE 100-METER GOLD AT THE 2012 OLYMPIC GAMES IN LONDON.

HEAD OVER HEELS CHINA'S QIN KAI FLIPS OUT MID-DIVE AT THE 2012 OLYMPIC GAMES.

A SWISS MAN
HOLDS THE RECORD FOR
HIGHEST DIVE:
HE *PLUNGED*
17 STORIES
INTO **A LAKE!**

SAY "CHEESE!"

WATER FIGHT GREAT BRITAIN'S ANGIE WINSTANLEY-SMITH KEEPS HER HEAD ABOVE WATER DURING A 2012 OLYMPIC GAMES WATER POLO MATCH.

LIFE-SIZE

RIO DE JANEIRO, BRAZIL

Forget soccer, the sport people packed into Rio to watch for the 2014 World Cup.
How much fun would it be to get inside this life-size foosball game? The giant table
debuted during the Carnival parade a few months prior to the World Cup games and
featured real people swinging around poles to kick an inflatable ball.

FOOSBALL

YOU PLAY WHAT?

Mix and Match

Old sports are old news. For something new and interesting, athletes have started combining sports to create wacky hybrid games with reimagined rules and arenas (one now popular example: Frisbee golf). Mix and match the sports shown to create your own outrageous new game, and then come up with your own set of rules. Check out the key to see if you've invented a brand-new sport or if the mix you made already exists!

FRISBEE + GOLF = FRISBEE GOLF

JOUSTING

CHESS

POLO

GOLF

SOCCER

UNICYCLING

CANOEING

BOXING

ANSWERS: UNICYCLE JOUSTING, UNICYCLE POLO, CHESS BOXING, CANOE POLO, AND SOCCER GOLF ARE ALL REAL HYBRID SPORTS!

CHAPTER 8

CULTURE SHOCK

G LAST NAME FINALLY FITS ID • WORLD'S TALL
ORD-SETTING ART • SEATTLE'S OWN SUPERHERO
CE PERFORMANCE • MAKING ART WITH ... BUGS!
K PLAYGROUNDS" BAN PARENTS • CRAZY CREAT
"BAN PARENTS • YOU WEAR THIS? • PROM

UNBELIEVABLE
BALLOON MAN,
PAGE 168

151

LONG LAST NAME *FINALLY* FITS ID

HONOLULU, HAWAII, U.S.A.

What's in a name? A lot of history and 19 syllables, for Hawaiian woman Janice Keihanaikukauakahihulihe'ekahaunaele. In 2013, she finally got her 36-character last name (35 letters and 1 *okina*, a mark used in the Hawaiian alphabet) to fit on her driver's license. The Hawaii Department of Transportation honored her request to allow longer names on licenses—now up to 40 characters for first and last names each, 35 for middle names.

SEATTLE'S OWN SUPERHERO?

WHO PHOENIX JONES

WHAT PATROLS CITY STREETS WHILE IN FULL SUPERHERO COSTUME, COMPLETE WITH FACE MASK AND AB-OUTLINED BODY ARMOR.

WHERE SEATTLE, WASHINGTON, U.S.A.

WHEN SINCE 2010

HOW THE SELF-PROCLAIMED "GUARDIAN OF SEATTLE" WANTS TO DO HIS PART IN KEEPING THE CITY'S RESIDENTS SAFE—WITHOUT BREAKING THE LAW. PHOENIX JONES AND HIS WIFE/SIDEKICK PURPLE REIGN GIVE OUT BLANKETS AND PONCHOS TO THE CITY'S HOMELESS, ORGANIZE NEIGHBORHOOD WATCH PROGRAMS, AND TAKE PHOTOS OR VIDEO OF CRIMES THEY HAPPEN TO SEE IN PROGRESS, SO THEY CAN HELP THE COPS MAKE AN ARREST. THEY'VE EVEN BEEN KNOWN TO RUN AFTER A BAD GUY OR TWO.

NEWS FEED

>>> **KAMPALA, UGANDA:** UGANDA RECENTLY GOT ITS FIRST AUTO BODY SHOP, AND CUSTOMERS ARE PAYING BIG BUCKS TO GIVE THEIR CARS CRAZY NEW

WORLD'S TALLEST, *FASTEST* WATERSLIDE OPENS

KANSAS CITY, KANSAS, U.S.A.

Fear fans will want to head to Kansas City ASAP for a ride on Verrückt, a frighteningly tall, superfast waterslide that opened in 2014. The three-person raft ride starts with a 264-step climb to the top. From there, riders plunge from a height higher than Niagara Falls and reach speeds of up to 65 miles and hour (105 km/h)! It's probably best to eat lunch *after* your ride.

WHOOOOOSH!

TURNING TRASH INTO RECORD-SETTING ART

DAMASCUS, SYRIA

Syrian artists found beauty in the form of a colorful mosaic made from cans, kitchen utensils, broken mirrors, and busted bike wheels. The 7,750-square-foot (720-sq-m) piece of artwork—the world's largest mural made of recycled materials—is displayed on the side of an elementary school. Students have said the mural makes them more excited to go to class!

LOOKS! STURDY FIBERGLASS CAN MAKE A CAR LOOK LIKE A CROCODILE, WHILE STILL WITHSTANDING KAMPALA'S POTHOLE-RIDDLED ROADS.

BAGS AS BALLERiNAS

LONDON, ENGLAND

These ghostly looking ballerinas are actually plastic bags!
Choreographer Phia Ménard uses wind machines to move her "dancers" in the musical production *L'Après-Midi d'un Foehn*, part of the 2014 London International Mime Festival. One human performer manipulates more than a dozen gravity-defying bags to float across the stage to a score by famous French composer Claude Debussy. Ménard's dance company, Compagnie Non Nova, is founded on the idea of "not new things, but in a new way." You won't ever look at your garbage the same way again!

MAKING ART
WITH ...

BUGS!

LOS ANGELES, CALIFORNIA, U.S.A.

Good thing Stephen R. Kutcher isn't afraid of bugs: He uses the tiny legs of living creepy-crawlies to create pretty paintings! The L.A.-based artist and biologist started collecting fireflies at age four. Now, he dips cockroaches, flies, beetles, and other insects in colorful paint before releasing them onto a blank canvas to make their mark. Don't worry: His nontoxic, water-based paints don't harm the insects or leave them permanently colored.

A FRENCH ARTIST USES OLD **CAR** AND **BICYCLE** PARTS TO BUILD **LIFELIKE** (THOUGH OVERSIZE) **SCULPTURES** OF **INSECTS.**

NEWS FEED

>>> **ISHINOMAKI, JAPAN:** AFTER THE TOHOKU EARTHQUAKE AND TSUNAMI CRUSHED THIS COASTAL JAPANESE CITY IN 2011, A SCULPTOR DECIDED TO HELP OUT IN HIS

THE TALLEST SAND CASTLE EVER CONSTRUCTED STOOD *FOUR* STORIES HIGH!

SAND!

SAN FRANCISCO, CALIFORNIA, U.S.A.

Artist Andres Amador has to work fast. He has only a few hours during low tide to carve his beautiful art in the California sand before waves wash it away. The huge sketches are made with several types of rakes and can be as big as 100,000 square feet (9,290 sq m). For the more complicated geometric designs, he sometimes uses a rope to guide his lines. Why create art that disappears so quickly? "It's fun!" he says.

THE WORLD'S *FASTEST CAMERA* TAKES 4.4 TRILLION IMAGES *PER SECOND.*

MUSIC!

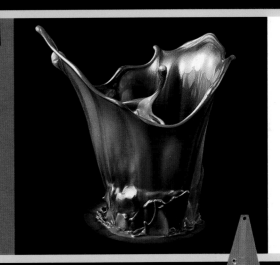

MARKTSTEINACH, GERMANY

Music from below, not a fall from above, made this paint jump! German artist Markus Reugels first sets up a puddle of paint and water on a balloon stretched over a speaker. He then plays techno music so low that the *thump-thump* of the bass makes the paint pulse. He creates cool prints like these by using high-speed photography to grab the exact moment the music moves the paint.

OWN WAY. WORKING WITH LOCAL SCHOOLKIDS WHO HAD BEEN AFFECTED BY THE TRAGEDY, TOGETHER THEY TURNED LEFT-BEHIND GARBAGE INTO COOL ARTWORK.

THERE ARE ROUGHLY **SEVEN QUINTILLION, FIVE HUNDRED QUADRILLION GRAINS OF SAND** ON **EARTH.**

WORLD'S FIRST SANDBOX

German Friedrich Froebel created the first sandbox, which back then was called a sand table or sand garden. He wanted to give children a place to dig, build, and explore. Froebel knows a thing or two about what kids like: He also invented kindergarten!

1847

>>> **PECULIAR MOMENTS IN PLAYTIME**

1923

SCARY SWINGS

What's wrong with this picture? This playground swing set may be one of Britain's first—but look how high swingers soar! Such heights and nothing soft beneath to break a fall would certainly be considered dangerous today. But back then, it was just another day at the park!

THE WORLD'S **TALLEST SWING,** ATTACHED TO THE **ROOF** OF A **SOCCER STADIUM** IN SOUTH AFRICA, IS MORE THAN **288 FEET** (88 M) **HIGH.**

"JUNK PLAYGROUNDS" BAN PARENTS

1943

In the 1940s, Danish architect Carl Theodor Sørensen noticed that kids bored easily at playgrounds and instead preferred junk piles or construction sites. So he invented the *skrammellegeplads*, or "junk playground," which featured some of the same building materials and the chance to make some pretty cool forts. A play leader supervised kids, but no parents were allowed!

DOWN 'N' DIRTY

2012

It's big, dirty, and disorganized, but kids in Wales love The Land. This acre of adventure includes things such as old tires, leftover furniture, thrown-away toys—all types of rubbish. There's even a creek, a fire pit, and a rope swing. It's a new version of the junk playground invented in the 1940s, giving kids freedom to create their own world with minimal adult supervision.

CRAZY CREATIONS

2003

Think your playground is cool? Check out these crazy creations in Denmark! In 2003, a company called Monstrum began building wooden playgrounds that look like giant spiders, angry robots, shipwrecked boats, and more. Each has its own story behind it.

CONTEST

BEAUTY IS IN THE EYE OF THE BEHOLDER

CAMELS HAVE **2 ROWS** OF **EYELASHES** THAT HELP KEEP **SAND** OUT OF THEIR **EYES.**

CAMELS CAN **DRINK** **30** GALLONS (114 L) OF WATER IN **13** MINUTES!

AL DHAFRA, UNITED ARAB EMIRATES

They've got long eyelashes and longer legs, but these lovely creatures aren't your typical beauty contestants. Every year, more than 25,000 camels (and their owners) descend on the desert outside Abu Dhabi for the Al Dhafra Festival, a pageant for the prettiest camels. And just what makes a camel good-looking? Judges prefer tall, purebred camels with a big head and feet and a wide, smooth neck. Firm ears, big whiskers, and a nice hump are also considered attractive.

The owners of the top beauties are the real winners: Prizes range from luxury cars to thousands of dollars in cash—and don't forget the bragging rights! Festivalgoers get to enjoy more than just the pageant; there's camel racing and camel milking, too!

FOR CAMELS

PAGEANT DAY PREP

JUDGES PREFER LONG LEGS.

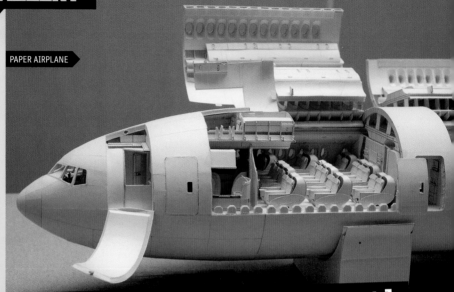

PAPER AIRPLANE

[CARD-BORED? DEFINITELY NOT!]

A little imagination can go a long way: These creative artists turned plain old cardboard into musical instruments, modes of transportation, monkeys, and more!

SORTA-POTTY

IT TAKES ABOUT
TWO MONTHS
FOR A CARDBOARD BOX TO
DECOMPOSE
IN A LANDFILL.

MONKEYING AROUND

MOTOR RE-CYCLE

A GROUP OF NEARLY

400
COLLEGE
STUDENTS USED MORE THAN
3,500 BOXES
TO BUILD A
CARDBOARD
FORT THAT **16** (4.9 M)
STOOD
FEET TALL.

GUITARS FROM GARBAGE

PRETTY PICTURES

WOULD YOU
WEAR THIS?

PROM QUEEN
(OF CANDY)

RIVER FALLS, WISCONSIN, U.S.A.

Most girls go out and buy a dress for their high school prom. But senior Tara Frey had a sweeter idea in mind—candy! Together with her mom, Tara spent more than 40 hours engineering her dress from collected Starburst candy wrappers, which they had folded eight times and then braided together over the years. While very cool, Tara admits the dress was not very comfortable. But at least she got to eat a lot of candy!

STARBURST CANDY WAS ORIGINALLY CALLED **OPAL FRUITS.**

NEWS FEED

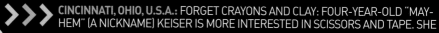

>>> CINCINNATI, OHIO, U.S.A.: FORGET CRAYONS AND CLAY: FOUR-YEAR-OLD "MAYHEM" (A NICKNAME) KEISER IS MORE INTERESTED IN SCISSORS AND TAPE. SHE

TRASHION
SHOW

VARIOUS LOCATIONS

These students love to recycle, reduce, and reuse—by creating wearable clothing from garbage! "Trashion" shows all over the world combine trash and fashion into one very cool event. These budding fashionistas use old food bags, computer parts, newspapers, and whatever else they can find to put together runway-worthy dresses such as this impressive kimono made of tea bags, coffee stirrers, garbage bags, and memory cards. Don't throw it, sew it!

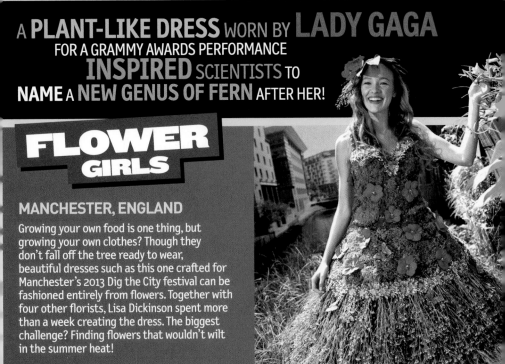

A **PLANT-LIKE DRESS** WORN BY **LADY GAGA** FOR A GRAMMY AWARDS PERFORMANCE **INSPIRED** SCIENTISTS TO **NAME** A **NEW GENUS OF FERN** AFTER HER!

FLOWER
GIRLS

MANCHESTER, ENGLAND

Growing your own food is one thing, but growing your own clothes? Though they don't fall off the tree ready to wear, beautiful dresses such as this one crafted for Manchester's 2013 Dig the City festival can be fashioned entirely from flowers. Together with four other florists, Lisa Dickinson spent more than a week creating the dress. The biggest challenge? Finding flowers that wouldn't wilt in the summer heat!

AND HER MOM MADE HEADLINES IN 2014 FOR MAKING REALISTIC PAPER VERSIONS OF CELEBRITIES' DRESSES AND DRESSES THAT HAD APPEARED IN FAIRY TALES AND ON T.V.

KiNG

GRAND RAPIDS, MICHIGAN, U.S.A.

You may have tried to solve a Rubik's Cube before, twisting and turning the brightly colored squares on each side to line them up. Artist Pete Fecteau plays with the cubes in a different way: He creates murals with them—4,242 of them, to be exact! His piece of art "Dream Big" (real big: it weighs 1,000 pounds/454 kg) is a portrait of civil rights activist Martin Luther King, Jr., constructed entirely from the cubes. Each was "solved" so that its colors line up in the correct pattern to make the giant mural come to life.

CUBED

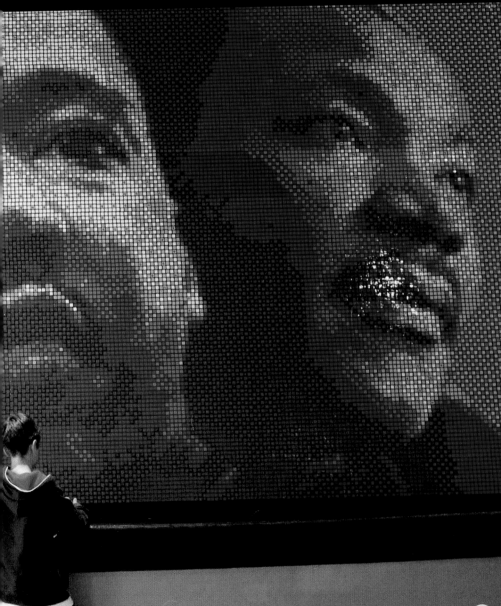

KNOW YOUR HERO

EVERY YEAR, ABOUT
130,000
SCIENCE FICTION, MOVIE,
AND COMIC BOOK FANS
(LIKE THESE SPIDER-MEN)
ATTEND **COMIC-CON**,
IN SAN DIEGO,
CALIFORNIA,
U.S.A.

How well can you identify a superhero by his or her awesome abilities? Test your knowledge by matching these comic book heroes with their special powers and magical gadgets. Check your answers in the key below. **》**

UNBELIEVABLE **BALLOON MAN** >>>

CLEVELAND, OHIO, U.S.A.

Did you know you can make your own superhero costume out of balloons? It may take hundreds of the long, twistable types (the same ones artists use to make fish, dogs, and other animals) and as long as ten hours, but Jeff Wright creates costumes of characters such as Iron Man and Buzz Lightyear that are big enough to wear!

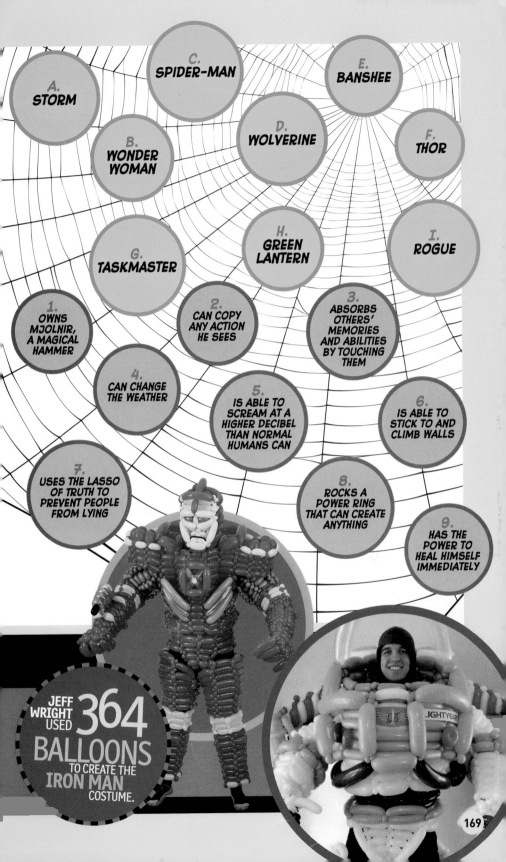

A. STORM

C. SPIDER-MAN

E. BANSHEE

B. WONDER WOMAN

D. WOLVERINE

F. THOR

G. TASKMASTER

H. GREEN LANTERN

I. ROGUE

1. OWNS MJOLNIR, A MAGICAL HAMMER

2. CAN COPY ANY ACTION HE SEES

3. ABSORBS OTHERS' MEMORIES AND ABILITIES BY TOUCHING THEM

4. CAN CHANGE THE WEATHER

5. IS ABLE TO SCREAM AT A HIGHER DECIBEL THAN NORMAL HUMANS CAN

6. IS ABLE TO STICK TO AND CLIMB WALLS

7. USES THE LASSO OF TRUTH TO PREVENT PEOPLE FROM LYING

8. ROCKS A POWER RING THAT CAN CREATE ANYTHING

9. HAS THE POWER TO HEAL HIMSELF IMMEDIATELY

JEFF WRIGHT USED **364** BALLOONS TO CREATE THE IRON MAN COSTUME.

LIGHTYEAR

INDEX

Illustrations are indicated by **boldface.**

CREDITS

FRONT COVER: (UPRT), Jim Zielinski/ Caters News Agency; (UP), Jimmy Chin/ National Geographic Creative; (CTR LE), Tomo Inukai of Watanoha Smile Project; (LO), Sol Neelman; **BACK COVER** (UPRT), Huang Bo/ChinaFotoPress/GettyImages; (LOLE), MattMarriott/BuschGardens/ Splash/Newscom; (LOCTR), NASA; (LORT), David Santiago Garcia/Getty Images; **SPINE:** Jimmy Chin/National Geographic Creative

FRONT MATTER: 1 (CTR), Robert Piper/ Caters News Agency; 2–3, Jimmy Chin/ National Geographic Creative; 5 (CTR), Greg Wolkins; 6–7 (CTR), Tina Anderson

CHAPTER 1: Wacky World Headlines
9 (CTR), NASA; 10–11 (CTR), AP Photo/ Markus Hell, Tareom.com, ho; 12 (UPRT), Nejron Photo/Shutterstock; 12 (CTR LE-cat), Andrey_Kuzmin/Shutterstock; 12 (CTR LE-tornado), Getty Images/ Willoughby Owen; 12 (CTR), vita khorzhevska/Shutterstock; 12 (LORT), © Michael Adkins; 13 (UPLE), AP Photo/Anne Ollila, Reindeer Herders' Association; 13 (CTR), © National Corvette Museum; 13 (CTR RT), © National Corvette Museum; 13 (LORT), Hiroshi Higuchi/Getty Images; 14–15 (Background), Elena Kharichkina/ Shutterstock; 14 (UP CTR), Claudia Naerdemann/Shutterstock; 14 (CTR), © Bob Dickerson; 14 (LORT), Jo Crebbin/ Shutterstock; 15 (UP CTR), © Hugh Chisholm; 15 (LORT), © STRINGER/MEXICO/ Reuters/Corbis; 16 (CTR), Giff Johnson/ AFP/Getty Images; 17 (UP CTR), STR/ AFP/Getty Images; 17 (LOLE), © iStock/ Roundhill; 17 (LO CTR), Life On White/ Getty Images; 17 (LORT), Franco Banfi/ Getty Images; 18 (CTR), Caters News Agency; 18 (LORT), Matteo Colombo/ Getty Images; 19 (UPLE), AP Photo/Reed College; 19 (CTR), Kazuhiro Nogi/AFP/Getty Images; 19 (LORT), Debstreasures/Getty Images; 20–21 (Background), © Wayne Edy, 2013; 21 (UPLE), © Wayne Edy; 21 (UPRT), © Ryan Edy; 22 (UP CTR), Caters News Agency; 22 (LO CTR), AP Images/ Kyodo; 22 (LORT), AP Photo/Foundation of Polish Modern Art; 23 (UPLE), © Fernando Guerra/Fotografia de Arquitectura; 23 (UP CTR), © Fernando Guerra/Fotografia de Arquitectura; 23 (UP), © Fernando Guerra/Fotografia de Arquitectura; 23

(UPRT), © Fernando Guerra/Fotografia de Arquitectura; 23 (CTR), © Lucas Brown; 23 (LO), Simon Dale/Caters New Agency; 24–25 (CTR), © Ema Peter, Courtesy Studio Echelman; 26, NASA/REX/AP; 27 (UPRT), NASA; 27 (LORT), photastic/ Shutterstock

CHAPTER 2: Wild Animals
29 (CTR), Aled Llywelyn/Caters News Agency; 30 (CTR), Hogle Zoo/AP Photo; 30 (LORT), Jim H Walling/Shutterstock; 31 (UP), Erik Rue/Caters News Agency; 31 (CTR), © Dr. Frank R. Rack, ANDRILL Science Management Office, University of Nebraska-Lincoln; 31 (LORT), Four Oaks/Shutterstock; 32–33 (Background), © Tim Laman/Caters News; 32 (LO), © Tim Laman/Caters News; 34 (CTR), Aled Llywelyn/Caters News Agency; 34 (LORT), Kerryn Parkinson/ZUMAPRESS/ Newscom; 35 (UP), Mary Krupa/Caters News Agency; 35 (CTR), sunsinger/ Shutterstock; 35 (LO), Caters News Agency; 36 (UP), © Europics/Newscom; 36 (LO), MattMarriott/BuschGardens/Splash/ Newscom; 37 (UPLE), Australia Zoo/Rex Features/AP Images; 37 (UPRT), 2014 Taronga Zoo/Getty Images; 37 (LOLE), National News/ZUMAPRESS/Newscom; 37 (LORT), © Steven Yensel/Staten Island Zoo; 38–39 (CTR) Matthew Horwood/ Caters News Agency; 40 (UP), Jagodka/ Shutterstock; 41 (UPRT), Tischenko Irina/ Shutterstock; 41 (LO), Kurt HP Guek/ NHPA/Photoshot/Newscom; 42 (ALL), The Phoenix Herpetological Society; 44–45 (Background), Yao tingshan/ Imaginechina/AP Images; 44 (UPLE), © Bettmann/Corbis; 44 (UPRT), Shawn Baldwin/AP Photo; 44 (LORT), Associated Press; 45 (UPRT), © Chaiwat Subprasom/ Reuters; 46 (CTR), © Tomas Persson; 46 (LO), © Mick Sibley; 47 (UP), M Evans/ Newspix/REX USA; 47 (CTR), Robert Piper/ Caters News Agency

CHAPTER 3: Incredible Inventions
48–49 (CTR), Jim Zielinski/Caters News Agency; 50 (UP), © J. Rogers, University of Illinois; 51 (UP), © Leif Ristroph; 51 (LO CTR), © Duncan Irschick, University of Massachusetts Amherst; 51 (LORT), © Duncan Irschick, University of Massachusetts Amherst; 52–53, Geoffrey Robinson/Rex/REX USA; 54–55

(Background), ©Hufton and Crow; 55 (UPRT), © Hufton and Crow; 56 (CTR), © Adam Voorhes; 56 (CTR RT), CB2/ZOB/ Supplied by WENN.com/Newscom; 57 (UP), © Remko de Waal/epa/Corbis; 57 (LO), Caters News Agency; 58–59 (Background), FPG/Hulton Archive/Getty Images; 58 (UPLE), © Hulton-Deutsch Collection/ Corbis; 58 (UPRT), © Bettmann/Corbis; 59 (UP), © Bettmann/Corbis; 59 (LO CTR), NASA; 60 (UPRT), © 3Doodler; 60 (CTR LE), © 3Doodler; 60 (LORT), BERPRESS/ Caters News Agency; 61 (UP), © Jonas Ingerstedt; 61 (LO CTR), Rex Features via AP Images; 62–63 (CTR), Mike Jones/ Caters News Agency; 64 (UP), © Baz Ratner/Reuters; 64 (LO), © Thomas de Wolf, Studio diip C.V.; 65 (UPLE), © Ethan Schlussler; 65 (UPRT), © RYNO Motors; 65 (LO CTR), Shepherd Zhou/FEATURECHINA/ Newscom; 66 (UP), © Marek Kowalski; 66 (LO), © Anna Flagg & Karon MacLean, SPIN Lab, UBC; 67 (UP), © Acquacalda/ Gianfranco Cignetti; 67 (LO), Jim Zielinski/ Caters News Agency

CHAPTER 4: Freaky Food
68–69 (LO), Ryan Gluesing; 70 (UP), Stefano Giovannini; 70 (LO), AP Photo/ The Oklahoman, Doug Hoke; 71 (UP), Natural Machines/Rex USA; 71 (CTR), Y. Liu and Y. Yang; 71 (LO), CB2/ZOB WENN Photos/Newscom; 72–73 (Background), Greg Wolkins; 72 (UP), Joe Zachariah; 72 (LO), Philip Weiss Auctions; 73 (UP), Soundwich; 74 (UPLE), REX USA/Mercury Press Agency; 74 (UPRT), REX USA/Clive Williams/Solent News/Rex; 74 (LOLE), newsteam.co.uk; 74 (LORT), Taylor Bowers/ Rex Features; 75 (UPLE), REX USA/Geoff Robinson; 75 (UPRT), REX USA; 75 (LOLE), newsteam.co.uk; 75 (LORT), REX USA/ Albanpix Ltd; 76–77 (ALL), Christopher Boffoli; 78–79 (UP), Solent News & Photo Agency; 80 (UPLE), Keith Tsuji/Getty Images; 80 (UPRT), Phant/Shutterstock; 80 (CTR), Keith Tsuji/Getty Images; 80 (LO), Ryan Gluesing; 81 (A), Martin Harvey/ Getty Images; 81 (B), Guillaume Meyer/ AFP/Getty Images; 81 (C), AP Photo/ Nick Ut, File; 81 (D), AP Photo/Nick Ut; 81 (E), Rex Features; 82–83, Tom Maddick/ Newsteam/SWNS Group; 84 (UP), Manny Hernandez/thetamalespaceship.com; 85 (UP), Rex USA; 85 (LO), AP Images/Wen bao-Imaginechina; 86 (Background), M.

Unal Ozmen/Shutterstock; 86 (1), Tim UR/ Shutterstock; 86 (2), MSPhotographic/ Shutterstock; 86 (3), StudioSmart/ Shutterstock; 86 (4), Tsekhmister/ Shutterstock; 86 (5-cheese), Givaga/ Shutterstock; 86 (5-pear), Tim UR/ Shutterstock; 86 (6), AdrianNunez/ Shutterstock; 86 (7), Schankz/ Shutterstock; 86 (8), B. and E. Dudzinscy/ Shutterstock; 86 (9), Jiang Hongyan/ Shutterstock; 86 (10), Catalin Petolea/ Shutterstock; 87 (UP), photastic/ Shutterstock; 87 (UP CTR), photastic/ Shutterstock; 87 (LO CTR), photastic/ Shutterstock; 87 (RT), M. Unal Ozmen/ Shutterstock; 87 (LO), Emilie Baltz

CHAPTER 5: Strange Science
89 (CTR), © Emily Baird; 90 (CTR), Javier Brosch/Shutterstock; 91 (UP), Michal Bednarek/Shutterstock; 91 (LO), © Emily Baird; 91 (LORT), Luke Peterson Photography/Getty Images; 92–93 (CTR), George Loegering/AP Photo; 94 (UP), © James I. Bingman; 94 (LO), © Norman Lim; 95 (UP), © Patricia Medici; 95 (CTR), © Goncalo M. Rosa; 95 (LORT), © Norman Lim; 96 (UP), Eric Isselee/ Life on White/SuperStock; 96 (LORT), gosphotodesign/Shutterstock; 97 (UP), milosljubicic/Shutterstock; 97 (LO), © Juniors/SuperStock; 98–99 (ALL), © Olivier Grunewald; 100–101 (Background), © Les Stocker/Getty Images; 100 (UPRT), Martin Palombini/moodboard; 100 (LO), Tsekhmister/Shutterstock; 101 (UPRT), Olaf Ballnus/Getty Images; 101 (LO), TechWizard/Shutterstock; 102–103 (ALL), © Jeff Cremer/PeruNature.com; 104 (UP), ROPI/ZUMA Press/Newscom; 104 (LO), © Galen Rowell/Corbis; 105 (UPRT), © Biosphoto/SuperStock; 105 (CTR LE), © Royal Saskatchewan Museum; 105 (CTR), Science Picture Co/Getty Images; 105 (LORT), Triff/Shutterstock; 106 (CTR), © Eye of Science/Science Source; 106 (LOLE), © Power and Syred/Science Source; 107 (UPRT), © Eye of Science/ Science Source; 107 (CTR LE), © Eye of Science/Science Source; 107 (CTR RT), © Andrew Syred/Science Source; 107 (LOLE), © SPL/Science Source

CHAPTER 6: Way-Out Travel
108–109 (LO), Hagen Hopkins/Getty Images; 110–111 (Background), Colin Brynn/Getty Images; 112 (UP), AP Images/ Imaginechina; 112 (LO), Shao Haijun/CHINE NOUVELLE/SIPA/Newscom; 113 (UP), Grady Coppell/Getty Images; 113 (LO), Emilio Naranjo/epa/Corbis; 114 (UP), Huang Bo/ ChinaFotoPress/GettyImages; 114 (LOLE), Paul Sakuma/AP; 114 (LORT), Handout/

MCT/Newscom; 115 (UP), Changi Airport Group/CB2/ZOB/WENN.com/Newscom; 115 (CTR LE), CB2/ZOB/WENN.com/Newscom; 115 (CTR RT), Roslan Rahman/AFP/ Getty Images; 115 (LO), Hagen Hopkins/ Getty Images; 116–117 (LO), limitezero. com; 116 (UP), Alhovik/Shutterstock; 116 (LO), erashov/Shutterstock; 117 (LE), erashov/Shutterstock; 117 (RT), Alhovik/ Shutterstock; 118 (UP), Thierry Roge/ Reuters/Corbis; 119 (UPLE), kiwi360; 119 (UPRT), Eak/Shutterstock; 119 (CTR), Andreas Rentz/Getty Images; 119 (LOLE), Michael Gottschalk/AFP/Getty Images; 119 (LORT), Raymond Walsh; 120–121 (Background), STR/AFP/Getty Images; 121 (UP), STR/AFP/Getty Images; 121 (CTR), STR/AFP/Getty Images; 121 (LO), China Daily/Reuters/Newscom; 122–123 (Background), BUS STOP/Alamy; 122 (UP), © Keystone Archives/HIP/The Image Works; 123 (UPLE), Jack Kurtz/ ZUMA Press/Corbis; 123 (UPRT), Volvo Car Group; 123 (LO), Danny Lawson/PA Wire URN:8330187 (Press Association via AP Images); 124 (UP), MelindaChan/Getty Images; 124 (LOLE), Alexander Ishchenko/ Shutterstock; 124 (LORT), Denis Burdin/ Shutterstock; 125 (UPLE), Keren Su/ Getty Images; 125 (UPRT), Paul & Paveena Mckenzie/Getty Images; 125 (LO), Frans Lanting; 126–127 (LO), Oscar Viñals; 128–129 (Background), ildogesto/Shutterstock; 128 (UP), Layne Kennedy/Corbis; 128 (LO), Zack Frank/Shutterstock; 129 (UPLE), Dominic Ebenbichler/Corbis; 129 (UPRT), David Santiago Garcia/Getty Images; 129 (LOLE), Aerostato/Shutterstock; 129 (LORT), Doug Houghton/Alamy

CHAPTER 7: Weird World of Sports
130–131, Sol Neelman; 132 (UP), Joshua Weisberg/Icon SMI CDB/Newscom; 132 (LO), AP Images/Johnny Quinn; 133 (UP), AP Images/Carlos Osorio; 133 (CTR LE), Carlos Osorio/AP/Corbis; 133 (CTR RT), Andrew Kelly/Reuters; 133 (LO), Namgyal Sherpa/AFP/Getty Images; 134–135 (LE), Cedar Wright; 135 (UP), Jimmy Chin/ National Geographic Creative; 135 (LO), Celin Serbo/Aurora Photos; 136–137 (CTR), Sol Neelman; 137 (UP), -1001-/iStockphoto; 137 (LO), Sol Neelman; 138 (UPLE), © Mike King/LNP/REX/Newscom; 138 (CTR), © Photo by Mike King/LNP/REX/Newscom; 139 (UP), Kevin T. Levesque/Getty Images; 139 (UPRT), Sol Neelman; 139 (LOLE), Tristan Savatier; 140–141 (Background), EPA/Kay Nietfeld/Alamy; 140 (UP), Al Bello/Allsport/Getty Images; 140 (LO), Central Press/Getty Images; 141 (UPLE), Streeter Lecka/Getty Images; 141 (UPRT), Jung Yeon-Je/AFP/Getty Images; 141

(CTR), Iryna Denysova/Shutterstock; 141 (LO), Brian Peterson/ZUMA Press/Corbis; 142–143 (Background), Sol Neelman; 143 (LO), Erika Shultz/The Seattle Times; 144 (UP), AP Images/Matt Slocum; 144 (LOLE), Teh Eng Koon/AFP/Getty Images; 144 (LORT), Greg Wood/AFP/Getty Images; 145 (UP), Quinn Rooney/Getty Images; 145 (CTR), Staff/Reuters; 145 (LO), AP Images/ Alastair Grant; 146–147 (LO), Celso Pupo/ Fotoarena/Sipa USA (Sipa via AP Images); 148 (UPLE), Artamonov Yury/Shutterstock; 148 (UP CTR), Andrew Rich/Getty Images; 148 (UPRT), Jari Hindstroem/ Shutterstock; 148 (LOLE), Robert H. Creigh/Shutterstock; 148 (LO CTR), Dennis W. Donohue/Shutterstock; 148 (LORT), Visage/Getty Images; 149 (UPLE), Cristian Lazzari/Getty Images; 149 (UPRT), Mitch Gunn/Shutterstock; 149 (CTR), Kumar Sriskandan/Alamy; 149 (LOLE), Lothar Knopp/Getty Images; 149 (LORT), Kazuhiro Nogi/AFP/Getty Images

CHAPTER 8: Culture Shock
150–151 (RT), Jeff Wright; 152 (UP), AP Images/Chris Stewart; 152 (LO), Austin Hargrave/AUGUST; 153 (UP), Charlie Riedel/AP/Corbis; 153 (CTR), Louai Beshara/AFP/Getty Images; 153 (LO), Louai Beshara /AFP/Getty Images; 154–155 (CTR), Murdo Macleod; 156 (UP), Steven Kutcher/Caters News Agency; 157 (UP), Simon Mildren; 157 (CTR), Markus Reugels; 157 (LO), Tomo Inukai of Watanoha Smile Project; 158–159 (Background), Monstrum/www.monstrum. dk; 158 (UP), Mary Evans Picture Library; 158 (LO), Geoffrey Robinson/Rex USA; 159 (UPLE), The Bridgeman Art Library; 159 (UPRT), Hanna Rosin/The Atlantic; 159 (LO), Monstrum/www.monstrum. dk; 160–161 (Background), Randy Olson/ National Geographic Creative; 161 (UP), Ali Haider/epa/Corbis; 161 (LO), Karim Sahib/AFP/Getty Images; 162 (UP), Luca Iaconi-Stewart; 162 (LOLE), **Don** Lucho/ Martin La Roche Contreras/Rex/Rex USA; 162 (LORT), James Grashow; 163 (UPLE), Chris Gilmour; 163 (UPRT), Kevin LCK/HotSpot; 163 (LORT), Kevin LCK/ HotSpot; 163 (LOLE), Chris Gilmour; 164 (UP), AP Images/Gina marrow; 165 (UP), CHINE NOUVELLE/SIPA/Newscom; 165 (CTR), Bates College; 165 (LO), CB2/ZOB/ Supplied by WENN.com/Newscom; 166 (UP), Popartic/Shutterstock; 166–167 (LO), Tina Anderson; 168–169 (UP), Vertyr/ Shutterstock; 168 (CTR), AP Images/ Joerg Carstensen/picture-alliance/dpa; 169 (LOLE), Jeff Wright; 169 (LORT), Jeff Wright

STAFF FOR THIS BOOK

Becky Baines, *Senior Editor*
Emily Krieger, *Project Editor*
Jay Sumner, *Photo Editor*
Jim Hiscott, *Art Director*
Alison Pearce Stevens and Chelsea Lin, *Writers*
Julie Beer and Michelle Harris, *Researchers*
Dawn Mcfadin and Rachel Hamm Plett, *Designers*
Chris Coffey and Margaret Sidlowsky, *Photo Researchers*
Sanjida Rashid and Rachel Kenny, *Design Production Assistants*
Colm Mckeveny, *Rights Clearance Specialist*
Grace Hill, *Managing Editor*
Mike O'Connor, *Production Editor*
Lewis R. Bassford, *Production Manager*
Nicole Elliott, *Manager, Production Services*
Susan Borke, *Legal and Business Affairs*

PUBLISHED BY THE NATIONAL GEOGRAPHIC SOCIETY

Gary E. Knell, *President and CEO*
John M. Fahey, *Chairman of the Board*
Melina Gerosa Bellows, *Chief Education Officer*
Declan Moore, *Chief Media Officer*
Hector Sierra, *Senior Vice President and General Manager, Book Division*

SENIOR MANAGEMENT TEAM, KIDS PUBLISHING AND MEDIA

Nancy Laties Feresten, *Senior Vice President;* Jennifer Emmett, *Vice President, Editorial Director, Kids Books;* Julie Vosburgh Agnone, *Vice President, Editorial Operations;* Rachel Buchholz, *Editor and Vice President,* NG Kids *magazine;* Michelle Sullivan, *Vice President, Kids Digital;* Eva Absher-Schantz, *Design Director;* Jay Sumner, *Photo Director;* Hannah August, *Marketing Director;* R. Gary Colbert, *Production Director*

DIGITAL

Anne McCormack, *Director;* Laura Goertzel, Sara Zeglin, *Producers;* Jed Winer, *Special Projects Assistant;* Emma Rigney, *Creative Producer;* Brian Ford, *Video Producer;* Bianca Bowman, *Assistant Producer;* Natalie Jones, *Senior Product Manager*

The National Geographic Society is one of the world's largest non-profit scientific and educational organizations. Founded in 1888 to "increase and diffuse geographic knowledge," the Society's mission is to inspire people to care about the planet. It reaches more than 400 million people worldwide each month through its official journal, *National Geographic,* and other magazines; National Geographic Channel; television documentaries; music; radio; films; books; DVDs; maps; exhibitions; live events; school publishing programs; interactive media; and merchandise. National Geographic has funded more than 10,000 scientific research, conservation, and exploration projects and supports an education program promoting geographic literacy.

For more information, please visit nationalgeographic.com, call 1-800-NGS LINE (647-5463), or write to the following address:
National Geographic Society
1145 17th Street N.W.
Washington, D.C. 20036-4688 U.S.A.

Visit us online at nationalgeographic.com/books

For librarians and teachers: ngchildrensbooks.org

More for kids from National Geographic:
kids.nationalgeographic.com

For information about special discounts for bulk purchases, please contact National Geographic Books Special Sales: ngspecsales@ngs.org

For rights or permissions inquiries, please contact National Geographic Books Subsidiary Rights: ngbookrights@ngs.org

Paperback ISBN: 978-1-4263-1909-9
Reinforced Library Binding ISBN: 978-1-4263-1910-5

Printed in the United States of America
15/QGT-CML/1